SOME YOU WIN

Some you don't

Compiled by
Wendy Body &
Pat Edwards

Acknowledgements

We are grateful to the following for permission to reproduce copyright material: Jonathan Cape Ltd on behalf of the author and illustrator for the poem 'Snow White and the Seven Dwarfs' from *Revolting Rhymes* by Roald Dahl, illustrated by Quentin Blake; Century Hutchinson Publishing Group Ltd for the story 'The Mixer' by P G Wodehouse; Andre Deutsch Ltd for the poem 'My Brother Gets Letters' from *Wouldn't You Like To Know* by Michael Rosen, illustrated by Quentin Blake; Faber & Faber Ltd for the story 'The Long Crawl' from *Dog Days and Cat Naps* by Gene Kemp; the author's agents for the story 'Had Yer Jabs?' by Max Fatchen from *Had Yer Jabs?* © Max Fatchen (pub Methuen Australia 1987); William Heinemann Ltd for the poem 'Praying Lion' in *Animal Fair* by Aidan Chambers; the author's agents for the poem 'My Week' from *Sky In The Pie* by Roger McGough (pub Kestrel Books); the author's agents for the story 'The Prince Rabbit' by A A Milne, Copyright A A Milne 1924. Pages 22-3 were written by Bill Boyle and Debbie Fox.

We are grateful to the following for permission to reproduce photographs: J Allan Cash, pages 24 *centre*, 25 *below left*, and *below right*; Genut, 28 Hertzog St, Givataim, Israel, page 50 *below*; The Jewish Museum, London, page 51 *left*; Gene Kemp, page 23; London Features International, page 24 *above*; Merseyside Tourism Board page 25 *above left* (photo R Jones), 25 *above right*; North Wales Picture Library, pages 24 *below*, 24/25 *background*; Sarah Shaps, page 51 *right*; Zefa, page 50 *above*.

Illustrators, others than those acknowledged with each story, include Rebecca Pannell pp.1-3 and 110-12; Dave Bowyer, title p.26; Rachel Senior pp.48-51; Jeannie Clark pp.52-3; Bettina Guthridge p.85.

Latest Betting

Contents

Snow-White and the Seven Dwarfs

When little Snow-White's mother died,
The king, her father, up and cried,
"Oh, what a nuisance! What a life!
Now I must find another wife!"
(It's never easy for a king
To find himself that sort of thing.)
He wrote to every magazine
And said, "I'm looking for a Queen".
At least ten thousand girls replied
And begged to be the royal bride.
The king said with a shifty smile,
"I'd like to give each one a trial".
However, in the end he chose
A lady called Miss Maclahose,
Who brought along a curious toy
That seemed to give her endless joy —
This was a mirror framed in brass,
A MAGIC TALKING LOOKING-GLASS.
Ask it something day or night,
It always got the answer right.
For instance, if you were to say,
"Oh Mirror, what's for lunch today?"
The thing would answer in a trice,
"Today it's scrambled eggs and rice".

4

Now every day, week in week out,
The spoiled and stupid Queen would shout,
"Oh Mirror Mirror on the wall,
Who is the fairest of them all?"
The Mirror answered every time,
"Oh Madam, you're the Queen sublime.
You are the only one to charm us,
Queen, you are the cat's pyjamas."
For ten whole years the silly Queen
Repeated this absurd routine.
Then suddenly, one awful day,
She heard the Magic Mirror say,
"From now on, Queen, you're *Number Two*.
Snow-White is prettier than you!"
The Queen went absolutely wild.
She yelled, "I'm going to scrag that child!
I'll cook her flaming goose! I'll skin 'er!
I'll have her rotten guts for dinner!"
She called the Huntsman to her study.
She shouted at him, "Listen buddy!
You drag that filthy girl outside,
And see you take her for a ride!
Thereafter slit her ribs apart
And bring me back her bleeding heart!"
The Huntsman dragged the lovely child
Deep deep into the forest wild.

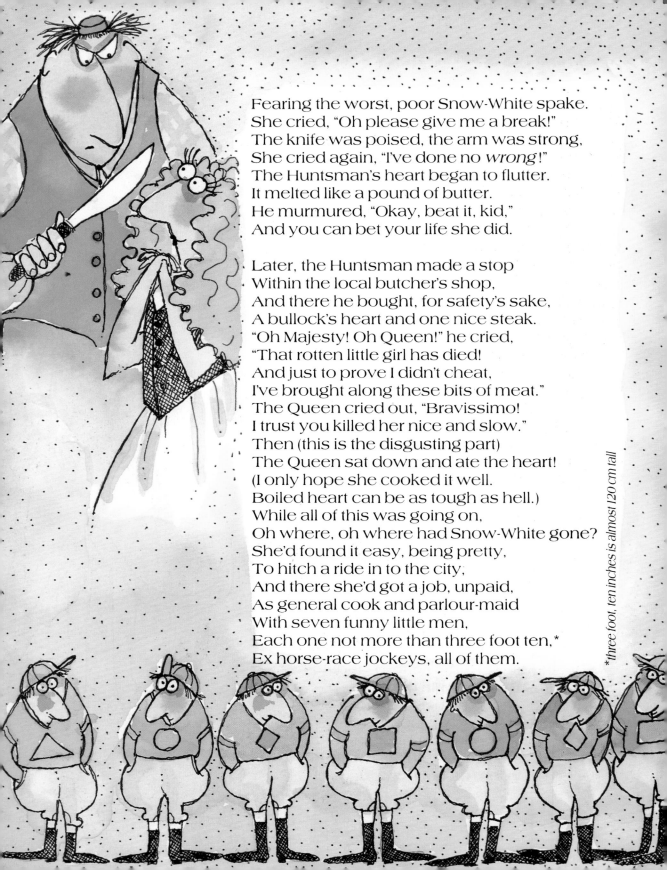

Fearing the worst, poor Snow-White spake.
She cried, "Oh please give me a break!"
The knife was poised, the arm was strong,
She cried again, "I've done no *wrong*!"
The Huntsman's heart began to flutter.
It melted like a pound of butter.
He murmured, "Okay, beat it, kid,"
And you can bet your life she did.

Later, the Huntsman made a stop
Within the local butcher's shop,
And there he bought, for safety's sake,
A bullock's heart and one nice steak.
"Oh Majesty! Oh Queen!" he cried,
"That rotten little girl has died!
And just to prove I didn't cheat,
I've brought along these bits of meat."
The Queen cried out, "Bravissimo!
I trust you killed her nice and slow."
Then (this is the disgusting part)
The Queen sat down and ate the heart!
(I only hope she cooked it well.
Boiled heart can be as tough as hell.)
While all of this was going on,
Oh where, oh where had Snow-White gone?
She'd found it easy, being pretty,
To hitch a ride in to the city;
And there she'd got a job, unpaid,
As general cook and parlour-maid
With seven funny little men,
Each one not more than three foot ten,*
Ex horse-race jockeys, all of them.

*three foot, ten inches is almost 120 cm tall

These Seven Dwarfs, though awfully nice,
Were guilty of one shocking vice —
They squandered all of their resources
At the race-track backing horses.
(When they hadn't backed a winner,
None of them got any dinner.)
One evening, Snow-White said, "Look here,
I think I've got a great idea.
Just leave it all to me, okay?
And no more gambling till I say."
That very night, at eventide,
Young Snow-White hitched another ride,
And then, when it was very late,
She slipped in through the Palace gate.
The King was in his counting house
Counting out his money,
The Queen was in the parlour
Eating bread and honey,
The footmen and the servants slept
So no one saw her as she crept
On tip-toe through the mighty hall
And grabbed THE MIRROR off the wall.

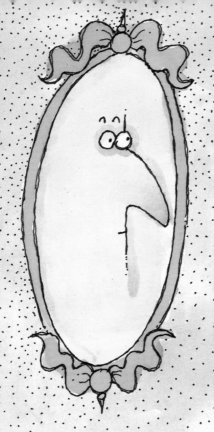

As soon as she had got it home,
She told the Senior Dwarf (or Gnome)
To ask it what he wished to know.
"Go on!" she shouted. "Have a go!"
He said, "Oh Mirror, please don't joke!
Each one of us is stony broke!
Which horse will win tomorrow's race,
The Ascot Gold Cup Steeplechase?"
The Mirror whispered sweet and low,
"The horse's name is Mistletoe".
The Dwarfs went absolutely daft,
They kissed young Snow-White fore and aft,
Then rushed away to raise some dough
With which to back old Mistletoe.
They pawned their watches, sold the car,
They borrowed money near and far,
(For much of it they had to thank
The manager of Barclays Bank.)
They went to Ascot and of course
For once they backed the winning horse.

8

Thereafter, every single day,
The Mirror made the bookies pay.
Each Dwarf and Snow-White got a share,
And each was soon a millionaire,
Which shows that gambling's not a sin
Provided that you always win.

Written by Roald Dahl
Illustrated by Rebecca Pannell

9

The Long Crawl

told by Lizzie Barnes

I twisted my ankle the evening before Sports Day, and I was
hopping mad about it, which is the only way you can be about
a twisted ankle, being both painful and unwanted, like a
rotten tooth. Furthermore it was not my fault at all, I was just
minding my own business, coming out of the fish and
chippery or the Chinese takeaway, depending on what you
fancy at the time, cod'n'chips or sweet and sour (I'd got
beefburgers), when Spider Hobbs, the mad brother of a friend
of mine, tripped me up in the doorway, so that I fell flat on
my face in the beefburgers, which, in a way, was a good thing
as my specs didn't break, but got instant grease instead, so
that I couldn't see, and I did not find it at all funny,
especially as the five thousand spectators did, and were
roaring their heads off, just like the Romans laughing at the
poor, suffering Christians in the Colosseum, and when I got
around to standing up there was this agony in my right foot,
and I could hardly walk. My friend, Jeff Hobbs, helped me
home, not far away, while I could hear Spider laughing fit to
burst behind me, and I thought, right, I'll get you later, but,
mainly, at the time, I was worrying about not being in the
Sports next day.

10

This worry proved only too correct. Despite Dad's efforts with cold compresses, witch hazel, and bandages, my foot swelled up and up to the size of a purple melon, and the person who was not going to win the high jump and the hundred metres was me. And believe me, before Spider and Fate tripped me up I stood a good chance. I won both last year, just beating Linda Holmes into second place, and though Patti Jones had arrived since then, I thought I could still win, despite her being nine metres high with legs to match. I tried to keep the bedclothes off my aching foot and cried.

We compete for houses, not ourselves, my house being Vikings — we won the Trophy last year, the others being Romans, Saxons, and Normans, boo, I can't stand the Normans, wish they'd never invaded us. From this you can see that our head teacher is a History fiend. There is a fair amount of rivalry about who is to get the Trophy this year.

Despite bandages from knee to toe, I was determined to go to school so as not to miss anything, and so Dad drove me to school, a rare treat, and delivered me up to our class teacher, Mr Higgins, who is a very nice man, and came with the school, I think, they have the same well-worn look. Dawn, my beautiful but dim friend, once asked him if it was frightening living at the time of the Black Death, and he said no, it wasn't as bad as living in a cave with the sabre-toothed tigers roaming about, so there is not much wrong with his humour, though Dawn believed every word and gave him the hideous knitted egg cosy she'd made, to make his life a bit comfier she said. Since egg cosies are one of the most useless things on the face of the earth, it didn't seem likely, but he thanked her kindly, and said it would make a big difference next time he was living in a cave.

Anyway, he was kind to me, too, when I crawled in, feeling about ninety-eight at the last birthday, and said that I could help him score so that I should not feel out of things, in fact, they were all kind to me, except Spider Hobbs and I did not speak to him. But I still felt mean and envious when I saw Linda and Patti in their kit, limbering up. Amongst the rest, this year there was to be a new athletics event, throwing the discus, and both of them were determined to win it.

I could tell you who was not going to win anything, who hates all Games and Sport, and who nearly drove me out of my mind that morning with moaning on and on, and that was my friend, Dawn.

"I didn't sleep last night," she began, during Maths.

"Neither did I," I replied, struggling with a work card on percentages, horrible things.

"It was my nerves," she went on.

"It was my foot."

"Oh, but you haven't got anything at all to worry about, since you've managed to get out of everything."

"But I didn't want to get out of anything."

"I think you're lucky."

"I don't."

"I can't bear to think of it. All those people watching."

"Don't worry. You can only came last."

"I don't want to disappoint my mother."

"Since you've come last in every race you've been in since you came to this school ages ago, she isn't likely to be disappointed this year. She must have got used to it."

"I don't think that's very nice, Lizzie Barnes. I might win something."

"Dawn, pigs might fly, and I might get this sum right, and you might win a race, but none of 'em are likely."

She turned her big blue eyes on me, hurt at such cruelty, but Mr Higgins suggested that it might be a good idea to do a little work for a change, and I was relieved to be quiet and ache and be miserable in peace. At play-time everyone jabbered away like mad about the Sports and I felt left out. My foot throbbed, so I grabbed a paperback on Heroes of the Past Who Achieved Great Things, and sat not reading, for my eyes seemed all gummed up although I wasn't crying. Patti came across and said in her soft voice, "It's not the same without you to run against," and I was just going to tell her how fed up I was, when Dawn joined us to say how scared she was of the obstacle race she was in, and that, at the last moment, to replace me, she'd been put down for throwing the discus. Some of us had some practice in this, but Dawn hardly knew what a discus was, let alone what to do with it.

In the afternoon we set off for the big sports field, about
half a mile away, that is, the whole school set off in a long trail
like a furry caterpillar in its green and yellow kit, and I drove
away in a car with the head teacher who was driving there to
see that everything was ready in advance. I felt peculiar and
grand driving past them all, and Spider Hobbs put out his
tongue, so I just stuck my nose in the air. At the field the head
teacher told me to hop up to the table where Mr Higgins was
to be scoring, so I crawled up to the stand and sat down
awkwardly at the edge of a chair, feeling like a twit, but the
school eventually churned into the field and each class sat
down in its place with its teachers and helpers. The air
buzzed with anticipation. Parents were arriving with small
brothers and sisters. Not mine. Mine were at work, and my
kid brother and sister were in the first school, which hadn't
come to this Sports — they have one of their own.

Sitting where I was between Mr Higgins and the head
teacher with the school loud-hailer, I had a good view of
everything, Linda and Patti, and Dawn, pale with terror. And
it seemed silly that she should be out there, having to do
something she didn't want to do, while I was perched up on a
stand, not doing what I wanted to.

Each house had its colour, Romans blue, Saxons yellow,
Vikings red, hooray, and Normans green, boo. Cards had
been made out with 1, 2 or 3 on them, and these were handed
to the winners as they arrived at the tape. The winners
brought them to me and I read them to Mr Higgins, who
totted up the score and wrote it on the score board.

The afternoon's events began, as they always did, with the
head teacher speaking gibberish through the loud-hailer — it
never works properly — first and second year before the
interval, third and fourth after. I felt mixed up about the
result. Of course I wanted my house to win, but I didn't want
it to do too well without me competing, so I finally decided
that I'd like them to win by one point with someone saying to
me, of course Vikings would have done better with you taking
part. That settled, everything started to happen quickly and I

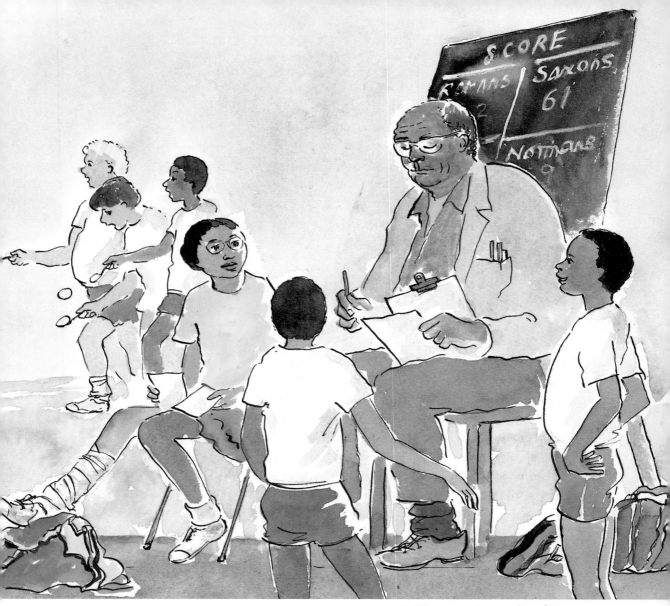

didn't have time to feel sorry for myself. The sun shone, but it wasn't too hot, and at half-time I was given a cup of tea with the staff and parents, which was super, except I did think as I nibbled one of Mr Higgins's biscuits that the ones who needed the refreshment most, the children, weren't getting any. By now, I felt like part of the staff and took no notice when Spider Hobbs made an excuse to come up to the stand and whisper 'Creepy Crawly, Lizzie Pawley' in my ear as it was so babyish.

By half-time the score was this: Romans 78, Saxons 75, Vikings 70 and Normans 61.

After the break, the Sports started up again, and now it grew more interesting as my friends were competing. When it was the fourth year's turn, Patti won the hundred metres, Linda the high jump, Patti the long jump, Jeff the boys' hundred metres, Spider the boys' hurdling — I hoped he'd catch his foot and fall over, but he didn't. And it was discus time. A dreadful, awful, ghastly and horrible boy called Walter J. Crow won the boys' event; then six girls took up positions, three in front, and the other three about six yards behind, Dawn in the front row, which didn't seem a good idea to me. She was wobbling like a blancmange, the rather slow and stately wobble she does when she is nervous, because it was her first event. Mr Higgins doesn't put her in track events any more, because she cannot keep in a lane and two years ago shot straight across the field, causing a pile-up, and Angie Bates had to be taken to the Outpatients. Remembering this, I wondered if Mr Higgins should have put her in the obstacle race, but he doesn't like leaving anybody out, just have a go and it doesn't matter he says.

Throwing a discus is a bit like hurling a flying saucer, the size of a plate but thicker. Dawn gripped hers, spun round and round, hurled it, and plonk, Linda Holmes is lying flat on

the ground. Dawn's discus had gone backwards instead of forwards. Proceedings were halted while Linda was revived and Dawn calmed, and the agitated parents settled once more. Finally, things began again, egg-and-spoon, sack, three-legged, won by Jeff and Spider, and the relay. Only the two obstacle races remained — they're always last because of the clearing away — and the score was now Romans 156 points, Vikings 154 points, Saxons 148 points, and Normans 139, hooray, they're last.

The obstacles were assembled and I was sorry I wasn't doing it instead of Dawn, who came up to the stand to ask if she could be let off, but Mr Higgins said she was the only girl Viking left available, so she went away agreeing — to her execution, from the sad look of her walking back to her place.

The course was hard. Balancing along an upturned form, handspring on a mat, ten-yard stretch with a skipping-rope, vault over the horse, jump through a hoop, leap over the box, throw three balls into a basket, pick out the last and crawl with it under a big black plastic tarpaulin, and run to the finishing-line.

Walter J. Crow won the boys' obstacle, yuck, then the girls lined up.

Dawn started off quite well, balancing on the form, despite wobbles. Handsprings were impossible but she rolled, getting a bit tangled up with her long hair, but struggling on with the skipping. Vaults had always proved a mystery to Dawn, but she hauled herself over gamely, though she was now in her usual place of last. And I found I was sitting there saying, Come on, old girl, you can do it, come on, Dawn, and willing her with every bit of my useless power just to get to the other end, because she was trying so hard when she didn't want to. Somehow she arrived at the tarpaulin, held down at the sides by lots of second-year feet. But as she struggled under, Angie Bates emerged at the other end and ran to the tape, and a great roar went up, for Angie and for Vikings, now ahead. One by one, the girls came out from under the plastic and Vikings had won by one point, and the crowd went mad, children starting to run all over the field and up to their parents. The second years holding down the tarpaulin were stamping up and down and yelling.

But I didn't care if we'd won, for Dawn was still under the tarpaulin. I'd watched and watched and knew she hadn't appeared. She'd be trampled to death!

I shouted to Mr Higgins but he didn't hear. I shouted even louder, but the noise was deafening.

I wished I could get to her. Curses on my ankle.

"Hello, horrible," bellowed a voice.

"Spider," I shrieked, "Dawn's still under there!"

"Right," he yelled back, and I forgave him my ankle — the lot — as he pushed through the crowd to find her.

On the table lay Mr Higgins's whistle. I picked it up and shoved it at him. He must have seen the look on my face, for he blew it, loud and long.

And silence fell.

And in the silence, her face mudstained, hair tangled, eyes enormous against the light, Dawn crawled out into the daylight, at the wrong end, the starting end, having turned completely round as she went. Spider, arriving panting beside her, yelled at the top of his voice:

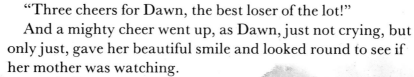

"Three cheers for Dawn, the best loser of the lot!"
And a mighty cheer went up, as Dawn, just not crying, but
only just, gave her beautiful smile and looked round to see if
her mother was watching.

Written by Gene Kemp
Illustrated by Pauline Little

We asked Gene Kemp to fill out this form because we wanted to know who had invented us.

MEET AN AUTHOR

Gene Kemp

Name:
Gene Kemp

Born in:
Wigginton, Tamworth, Staffordshire
(place, date)
1066 AD

Started school at:
Wigginton School

Favourite subject at school:
Reading

What I didn't like about school:
Having to stop reading

Favourite food when young:
Roast pork, apple sauce, roast potatoes, fish and chips,
strawberries, ice-cream, apple pie, chocolates, fudge.

Favourite food now:
The lot. No, wait a bit.

I don't really like macaroni cheese...

Best-loved story or book when young:
Wind in the Willows
William
The Rose & the Ring (bet you don't know that one)

Favourite kind of book now:
The lot. No, wait a bit. I don't much like spy stories or
romantic stories. Funny, ghosty thrillers best.

First book published by you:
The Prince of Tamworth Pig

Three things I like:
My cat Scroggins (our cat really)
My granddaughter, Rosanna
My little, littlest granddaughter, Emily

Three things I hate:
Cat Scroggins when he catches birds (and filling in forms like this).
Slugs(and filling in forms like this).
Shouty people on TV(and filling in forms like this).

Secret wish:
That other wishes would come true. The wish I've made about the
person who made me fill in this form is very, very interesting.
Especially if it comes true!! Ho, ho, hoho.

Favourite riddle/joke/cartoon:
What should you do
when you see
Frankenstein's monster,
four werewolves,
two vampires and
the Incredible Hulk
all in one room?

Keep your
fingers crossed and
hope that it's a
fancy dress party!

YER ALRIGHT SCOUSE

IT'S MY HOME

LIVERPOOL

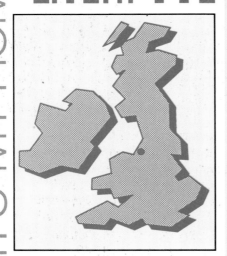

One thing Liverpool is well known for is its distinctive accent. Liverpudlians are known as scousers.

Julie Walters

Liverpool Playhouse

Liverpudlians have a keen sense of humour, and quite a few comedians come from Liverpool — Julie Walters, for instance. Playwrights like Willy Russell and Alan Bleasdale grew up in Liverpool. And what about music? Everybody has heard of The Beatles who were (and still are!) world-famous. The Beatles based some of their songs on actual locations in Liverpool, like Penny Lane and Strawberry Fields. Here is a statue of The Beatles by John Doubleday. It stands outside the Cavern Walks Shopping Centre, where The Cavern Club once stood. The Beatles played at that club 292 times.

Do you know any other bands or musicians from Liverpool?

There is quite high unemployment in Liverpool. Years ago the port of Liverpool brought much business and money into the city. As in other cities in the United Kingdom, the ports do not have the life they once had. Some are rebuilt as tourist centres. The Albert Dock in Liverpool was once a thriving working dock. It still thrives, but now from the business of tourism. These two photographs show how much the dock has changed; the first photograph is from the Museum of Labour History. The second is the dock today. The museum records, through photographs and objects, how life has changed for the working population since 1840.

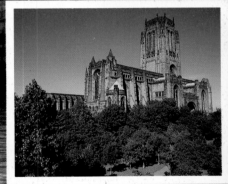

**Metropolitan Cathedral —
very modern structure**

**Anglican Cathedral —
largest Anglican cathedral in
the World**

A view of Liverpool from the water

THE
MIXER

THE BEST · EVER · THE BEST · EVER

P.G.WODEHOUSE

ALE

LOOKING BACK, I always consider that my career as a dog proper really started when I was bought for the sum of half a crown by the Shy Man. That event marked the end of my puppyhood. The knowledge that I was worth actual cash to somebody filled me with a sense of new responsibilities. It sobered me. Besides, it was only after that half-crown* changed hands that I went out into the great world; and, however interesting life may be in an East End public-house, it is only when you go out into the world that you really broaden your mind and begin to see things.

Within its limitations, my life had been singularly full and vivid. I was born, as I say, in a public-house in the East End, and however lacking a public-house may be in refinement and the true culture, it certainly provides plenty of excitement. Before I was six weeks old, I had upset three policemen by getting between their legs when they came round to the side-door, thinking they had heard suspicious noises; and I can still recall the interesting sensation of being chased seventeen times round the yard with a broom-handle after a well-planned and completely successful raid on the larder.

The Shy Man came into our yard one afternoon in April, while I was sleeping with mother in the sun on an old sweater which we had borrowed from Fred, one of the barmen. I heard mother growl, but I didn't take any notice. Mother is what they call a good watch-dog, and she growls at everybody except master. At first, when she used to do it, I would get up and bark my head off, but not now. Life's too short to bark at everybody who comes into our yard. It is behind the public-house, and they keep empty bottles and things there, so people are always coming and going.

Besides, I was tired. I had had a very busy morning, helping the men bring in a lot of cases of beer, and running into the saloon to talk to Fred and generally looking after things. So I was just dozing off again, when I heard a voice say, "Well, he's ugly enough!" Then I knew that they were talking about me.

---

* A coin worth 12½p now, but worth a lot more at the time of this story.

27

I have never disguised it from myself, and nobody has ever disguised it from me, that I am not a handsome dog. Even mother never thought me beautiful. She was no Gladys Cooper herself, but she never hesitated to criticize my appearance. In fact, I have yet to meet anyone who did. The first thing strangers say about me is, "What an ugly dog!"

I don't know what I am. I have a bulldog kind of a face, but the rest of me is terrier. I have a long tail which sticks straight up in the air. My hair is wiry. My eyes are brown. I am jet black, with a white chest. I once overheard Fred saying that I was a Gorgonzola cheese-hound, and I have generally found Fred reliable in his statements.

When I found that I was under discussion, I opened my eyes. Master was standing there, looking down at me, and by his side the man who had just said I was ugly enough. The man was a thin man, about the age of a barman and smaller than a policeman. He had patched brown shoes and black trousers.

"But he's got a sweet nature," said master.

This was true, luckily for me. Mother always said, "A dog without influence or private means, if he is to make his way in the world, must have either good looks or amiability." But, according to her, I overdid it. "A dog," she used to say, "can have a good heart, without chumming with every Tom, Dick, and Harry he meets. Your behaviour is sometimes quite un-doglike." Mother prided herself on being a one-man dog. She kept herself to herself, and wouldn't kiss anybody except master — not even Fred.

Now, I'm a mixer. I can't help it. It's my nature. I like men. I like the taste of their boots, the smell of their legs, and the sound of their voices. It may be weak of me, but a man has only to speak to me and a sort of thrill goes right down my spine and sets my tail wagging.

I wagged it now. The man looked at me rather distantly. He didn't pat me. I suspected — what I afterwards found to be the case — that he was shy, so I jumped up at him to put him at his ease. Mother growled again. I felt that she did not approve.

"Why, he's took quite a fancy to you already," said master.

The man didn't say a word. He seemed to be brooding on something. He was one of those silent men. He reminded me of Joe, the old dog down the street at the grocer's shop, who lies at the door all day, blinking and not speaking to anybody.

Master began to talk about me. It surprised me, the way he praised me. I hadn't a suspicion he admired me so much. From what he said you would have thought I had won prizes and ribbons at the Crystal Palace. But the man didn't seem to be impressed. He kept on saying nothing.

When master had finished telling him what a wonderful dog I was till I blushed, the man spoke.

"Less of it," he said. "Half a crown is my bid, and if he was an angel from on high you couldn't get another ha'penny* out of me. What about it?"

* A coin worth less than ½p now!

A thrill went down my spine and out at my tail, for of course I saw now what was happening. The man wanted to buy me and take me away. I looked at master hopefully.

"He's more like a son to me than a dog," said master, sort of wistful.

"It's his face that makes you feel that way," said the man, unsympathetically. "If you had a son that's just how he would look. Half a crown is my offer, and I'm in a hurry."

"All right," said master, with a sigh, "though it's giving him away, a valuable dog like that. Where's your half-crown?"

The man got a bit of rope and tied it round my neck. I could hear mother barking advice and telling me to be a credit to the family, but I was too excited to listen.

"Goodbye mother," I said. "Goodbye, master. Goodbye Fred. Goodbye everybody. I'm off to see life. The Shy Man has bought me for half a crown. Wow!"

I kept running round in circles and shouting, till the man gave me a kick and told me to stop it. So I did.

I don't know where we went, but it was a long way. I had never been off our street before in my life and I didn't know the whole world was half as big as that. We walked on and on, the man jerking at my rope whenever I wanted to stop and look at anything. He wouldn't even let me pass the time of the day with dogs we met.

When we had gone about a hundred miles and were just going to turn in at a dark doorway, a policeman suddenly stopped the man. I could feel by the way the man pulled at my rope and tried to hurry on that he didn't want to speak to the policeman. The more I saw of the man, the more I saw how shy he was.

"Hi!" said the policeman, and we had to stop.

"I've got a message for you, old pal," said the policeman. "It's from the Board of Health. They told me to tell you you needed a change of air. See?"

"All right!" said the man.

"And take it as soon as you like. Else you'll find you'll get it given you. See?"

I looked at the man with a good deal of respect. He was evidently someone important, if they worried so about his health.

"I'm going down to the country tonight," said the man.

The policeman seemed pleased.

"That's a bit of luck for the country," he said. "Don't go changing your mind."

And we walked on, and went in at the dark doorway, and climbed about a million stairs and went into a room that smelt of rats. The man sat down and swore a little, and I sat and looked at him. Presently I couldn't keep it in any longer.

"Do we live here?" I said. "Is it true we're going to the country? Wasn't that policeman a good sort? Don't you like policemen? I knew lots of policemen at the public-house. Are there any other dogs here? What is there for dinner? What's in that cupboard? When are you going to take me out for another

run? May I go out and see if I can find a cat?"

"Stop that yelping," he said.

"When we go to the country, where shall we live? Are you going to be caretaker at a house? Fred's father is a caretaker at a big house in Kent. I've heard Fred talk about it. You didn't meet Fred when you came to the public-house, did you? You would like Fred. I like Fred. Mother likes Fred. We all like Fred."

I was going to tell him a lot more about Fred, who had always been one of my warmest friends, when he suddenly got hold of a stick and walloped me with it.

"You keep quiet when you're told," he said.

He really was the shyest man I had ever met. It seemed to hurt him to be spoken to. However, he was the boss, and I had to humour him, so I didn't say any more.

We went down to the country that night, just as the man had told the policeman we would. I was all worked up, for I had heard so much about the country from Fred that I had always wanted to go there. Fred used to go off on a motor-bicycle sometimes to spend the night with his father in Kent, and once he brought back a squirrel with him, which I thought was for me to eat, but mother said no. "The first thing a dog has to learn," mother used often to say, "is that the whole world wasn't created for him to eat."

It was quite dark when we got to the country, but the man seemed to know where to go. He pulled at my rope, and we began to walk along a road with no people in it at all. We walked on and on, but it was all so new to me that I forgot how tired I was.

Every now and then we would pass a very big house, which looked as if it was empty, but I knew that there was a caretaker inside, because of Fred's father. These big houses belong to very rich people, but they don't want to live in them till the summer, so they put in caretakers, and the caretakers have a dog to keep off burglars. I wondered if that was what I had been brought here for.

"Are you going to be a caretaker?" I asked the man.

"Shut up," he said.

So I shut up.

After we had been walking a long time, we came to a cottage. A man came out. My man seemed to know him, for he called him Bill. I was quite surprised to see the man was not at all shy with Bill. They seemed very friendly.

"Is that him?" said Bill, looking at me.

"Bought him this afternoon," said the man.

"Well," said Bill, "he's ugly enough. He looks fierce. If you want a dog, he's the sort of dog you want. But what do you want one for? It seems to me it's a lot of trouble to take, when there's no need of any trouble at all. Why not do what I've always wanted to do? What's wrong with just fixing the dog, same as it's always done, and walking in and helping yourself?"

"I'll tell you what's wrong," said the man. "To start with, you can't get at the dog and fix him except by day, when they let him out. At night he's shut up inside the house. And suppose you do fix him during the day, what happens then? Either the bloke gets another before night, or else he sits up all night with a gun. It isn't like as if these blokes was ordinary blokes. They're down here to look after the house. That's their job, and they don't take any chances."

It was the longest speech I had ever heard the man make, and it seemed to impress Bill. He was quite humble.

"I didn't think of that," he said. "We'd best start in to train this tyke at once."

Mother often used to say, when I went on about wanting to go out into the world and see life, "You'll be sorry when you do. The world isn't all bones and liver."

And I hadn't been living with the man and Bill in their cottage long before I found out how right she was. It was the man's shyness that made all the trouble. It seemed as if he hated to be taken notice of.

It started on my very first night at the cottage. I had fallen asleep in the kitchen, tired out after all the excitement of the day and the long walks I had had, when something woke me with a start. It was somebody scratching at the window, trying to get in.

Well, I ask you, I ask any dog, what would you have done in my place? Ever since I was old enough to listen, mother had told me over and over again what I must do in a case like this. It is the A B C of a dog's education. "If you are in a room and you hear anyone trying to get in," mother used to say, "bark. It may be someone who has business there, or it may not. Bark first, and inquire afterwards. Dogs were made to be heard and not seen."

I lifted my head and yelled. I have a good, deep voice, due to a hound strain in my pedigree, and at the public-house,

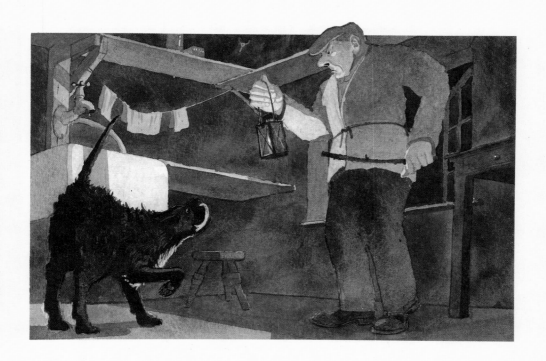

when there was a full moon, I have often had people leaning out of the windows and saying things all down the street. I took a deep breath and let it go.

"Man!" I shouted. "Bill! Man! Come quick! Here's a burglar getting in!"

Then somebody struck a light, and it was the man himself. He had come in through the window. He picked up a stick, and he walloped me. I couldn't understand it. I couldn't see where I had done the wrong thing. But he was the boss, so there was nothing to be said.

If you'll believe me, that same thing happened every night. Every single night! And sometimes twice or three times before morning. And every time I would bark my loudest, and the man would strike a light and wallop me. The thing was baffling. I couldn't possibly have mistaken what mother had said to me. She said it too often for that. Bark! Bark! Bark! It was the main plank of her whole system of education. And yet, here I was, getting walloped every night for doing it.

I thought it out till my head ached, and finally I got it right.

I began to see that mother's outlook was narrow. No doubt, living with a man like master at the public-house, a man without a trace of shyness in his composition, barking was all right. But circumstances alter cases. I belonged to a man who was a mass of nerves, who got the jumps if you spoke to him. What I had to do was to forget the training I had had from mother, sound as it no doubt was as a general thing, and to adapt myself to the needs of the particular man who had happened to buy me. I had tried mother's way, and all it had brought me was walloping, so now I would think for myself.

So next night, when I heard the window go, I lay there without a word, though it went against all my better feelings. I didn't even growl. Someone came in and moved about in the dark, with a lantern, but, though I smelt that it was the man, I didn't ask him a single question. And presently the man lit a light and came over to me and gave me a pat, which was a thing he had never done before.

"Good dog!" he said. "Now you can have this."

And he let me lick out the saucepan in which the dinner had been cooked. After that, we got on fine. Whenever I heard anyone at the window I just kept curled up and took no notice, and every time I got a bone or something good. It was easy, once you had got the hang of things.

It was about a week after that the man took me out one morning, and we walked a long way till we turned in at some big gates and went along a very smooth road till we came to a great house, standing all by itself in the middle of a whole lot of country. There was a big lawn in front of it, and all round there were fields and trees, and at the back a great wood.

The man rang a bell, and the door opened, and an old man came out.

"Well?" he said, not very cordially.

"I thought you might want to buy a good watchdog," said the man.

"Well, that's queer, your saying that," said the caretaker.

"It's a coincidence. That's exactly what I do want to buy. I was just thinking of going along and trying to get one. My old dog picked up something this morning that he oughtn't to have, and he's dead, poor feller."

"Poor feller," said the man. "Found an old bone with phosphorus on it, I guess."

"What do you want for this one?"

"Five shillings."

"Is he a good watchdog?"

"He's a grand watchdog."

"He looks fierce enough."

"Ah!"

So the caretaker gave the man his five shillings, and the man went off and left me.

At first the newness of everything and the unaccustomed

smells and getting to know the caretaker, who was a nice old man, prevented my missing the man, but as the day went on and I began to realize that he'd gone and would never come back, I got very depressed. I pattered all over the house, whining. It was a most interesting house, bigger than I thought a house could possibly be, but it couldn't cheer me up. You may think it strange that I should pine for the man, after all the wallopings he had given me, and it is odd, when you come to think of it. But dogs are dogs, and they are built like that. By the time it was evening I was thoroughly miserable. I found a shoe and an old clothes-brush in one of the rooms, but could eat nothing. I just sat and moped.

It's a funny thing, but it seems as if it always happens that just when you are feeling most miserable, something nice happens. As I sat there, there came from outside the sound of a motor-bicycle, and somebody shouted.

It was dear old Fred, my old pal Fred, the best old boy that ever stepped. I recognized his voice in a second, and I was scratching at the door before the old man had time to get up out of his chair. Well, well, well! That was a pleasant surprise! I ran five times round the lawn without stopping, and then I came back and jumped up at him.

"What are you doing here, Fred?" I said. "Is this caretaker your father? Have you seen the rabbits in the wood? How long are you going to stop? How's mother? I like the country. Have you come all the way from the public-house? I'm living here now. Your father gave five shillings* for me. That's twice as much as I was worth when I saw you last."

"Why, it's young Bouncer!" That was what they called me at the saloon. "What are you doing here? Where did you get this dog, father?"

"A man sold him to me this morning. Poor old Bob got poisoned. This one ought to be just as good a watchdog. He barks loud enough."

"He should be. His mother is the best watchdog in London. This cheese-hound used to belong to the boss. Funny him getting down here."

* Worth 25p now.

We went into the house and had supper. And after supper we sat and talked. Fred was only down for the night, he said, because the boss wanted him back next day.

"And I'd sooner have my job, than yours, dad," he said. "Of all the lonely places! I wonder you aren't scared of burglars."

"I've my shot-gun, and there's the dog. I might be scared if it wasn't for him, but he kind of gives me confidence. Old Bob was the same. Dogs are a comfort in the country."

"Get many tramps here?"

"I've only seen one in two months, and that's the feller who sold me the dog here."

As they were talking about the man, I asked Fred if he knew him. They might have met at the public-house, when the man was buying me from the boss.

"You would like him," I said. "I wish you could have met."

"What's he growling at?" asked Fred. "Think he heard something?"

The old man laughed.

"He wasn't growling. He was talking in his sleep. You're nervous, Fred. It comes of living in the city."

"Well, I am. I like this place in the daytime, but it gives me the pip at night. It's so quiet. How you can stand it here all the time, I can't understand. Two nights of it would have me seeing things."

His father laughed.

"If you feel like that, Fred, you had better take the gun to bed with you. I shall be quite happy without it."

"I will," said Fred. "I'll take six if you've got them."

And after that they went upstairs. I had a basket in the hall, which had belonged to Bob, the dog who had got poisoned. It was a comfortable basket, but I was so excited at having met Fred again that I couldn't sleep. Besides, there was a smell of mice somewhere, and I had to move around, trying to place it.

I was just sniffing at a place in the wall, when I heard a scratching noise. At first I thought it was the mice working in a different place, but, when I listened, I found that the sound came from the window. Somebody was doing something to it from the outside.

If it had been mother, she would have lifted the roof off right there, and so should I, if it hadn't been for what the man had taught me. I didn't think it possible that this could be the man come back, for he had gone away and said nothing about ever seeing me again. But I didn't bark. I stopped where I was and listened. And presently the window came open, and somebody began to climb in.

I gave a good sniff, and I knew it was the man. I was so delighted that for a moment I nearly forgot myself and shouted with joy, but I remembered in time how shy he was, and stopped myself. But I ran to him and jumped up quite quietly, and he told me to lie down. I was disappointed that he didn't seem more pleased to see me. I lay down.

It was very dark, but he had brought a lantern with him, and I could see him moving about the room, picking things up and putting them in a bag which he had brought with him. Every now and then he would stop and listen, and then he would start moving round again. He was very quick about it, but very quiet. It was plain that he didn't want Fred or his father to come down and find him.

I kept thinking about this peculiarity of his while I watched him. I suppose, being chummy myself, I find it hard to understand that everybody else in the world isn't chummy too. Of course, my experience at the public-house had taught me that men are just as different from each other as dogs. If I chewed master's shoe, for instance, he used to kick me; but if I chewed Fred's, Fred would tickle me under the ear. And, similarly, some men are shy and some men are mixers. I quite appreciated that, but I couldn't help feeling that the man carried shyness to a point where it became morbid. And he didn't give himself a chance to cure himself of it. That was the point. Imagine a man hating to meet people so much that he never visited their houses till the middle of the night, when they were in bed and asleep. It was silly. Shyness has always been something so outside my nature that I suppose I have

never really been able to look at it sympathetically. I have always held the view that you can get over it if you make an effort. The trouble with the man was that he wouldn't make an effort. He went out of his way to avoid meeting people.

I was fond of the man. He was the sort of person you never got to know very well, but we had been together for quite a while, and I wouldn't have been a dog if I hadn't got attached to him.

As I sat and watched him creep about the room, it suddenly came to me that here was a chance of doing him a real good turn in spite of himself. Fred was upstairs, and Fred, as I knew by experience, was the easiest man to get along with in the world. Nobody could be shy with Fred. I felt that if only I could bring him and the man together, they would get along splendidly, and it would teach the man not to be silly and avoid people. It would help to give him the confidence which he needed. I had seen him with Bill, and I knew that he could be perfectly natural and easy when he liked.

It was true that the man might object at first, but after a while he would see that I had acted simply for his good, and would be grateful.

The difficulty was, how to get Fred down without scaring the man. I knew that if I shouted he wouldn't wait, but would be out of the window and away before Fred could get there. What I had to do was to go to Fred's room, explain the whole situation quietly to him, and ask him to come down and make himself pleasant. The man was far too busy to pay any attention to me. He was kneeling in a corner with his back on me, putting something in his bag. I seized the opportunity to steal softly from the room.

Fred's door was shut, and I could hear him snoring. I scratched gently, and then harder, till I heard the snores stop. He got out of bed and opened the door.

"Don't make a noise," I whispered. "Come on downstairs. I want you to meet a friend of mine."

At first he was quite peevish.

"What's the idea," he said, "coming and spoiling a man's

beauty-sleep? Get out."

He actually started to go back into the room.

"No, honestly, Fred," I said, "I'm not fooling you. There is a man downstairs. He got in through the window. I want you to meet him. He's very shy, and I think it will do him good to have a chat with you."

"What are you whining about?" Fred began, and then he broke off suddenly and listened. We could both hear the man's footsteps as he moved about.

Fred jumped back into the room. He came out carrying something. He didn't say any more, but started to go downstairs, very quiet, and I went after him.

There was the man, still putting things in his bag. I was just going to introduce Fred, when Fred, the silly ass, gave a great yell. I could have bitten him.

"What did you want to do that for, you chump?" I said. "I told you he was shy. Now you've scared him."

He certainly had. The man was out of the window quicker than you would have believed possible. He just flew out. I called after him that it was only Fred and me, but at that moment a gun went off with a tremendous bang, so he couldn't have heard me.

I was pretty sick about it. The whole thing had gone wrong. Fred seemed to have lost his head entirely. He was behaving like a perfect ass. Naturally the man had been frightened with him carrying on in that way. I jumped out of the window to see if I could find the man and explain, but he was gone. Fred jumped out after me, and nearly squashed me.

It was pitch dark out there. I couldn't see a thing. But I knew the man could not have gone far, or I should have heard him. I started to sniff round on the chance of picking up his trail. It wasn't long before I struck it.

Fred's father had come down now, and they were running about. The old man had a light. I followed the trail, and it ended at a large cedar-tree, not far from the house. I stood underneath it and looked up, but of course I could not see anything.

"Are you up there?" I shouted. "There's nothing to be scared at. It was only Fred. He's an old pal of mine. He works at the place where you bought me. His gun went off by accident. He won't hurt you."

There wasn't a sound. I began to think I must have made a mistake.

"He's got away," I heard Fred say to his father and, just as
he said it I caught a faint sound of someone moving in the
branches above me.

"No he hasn't!" I shouted. "He's up this tree."

"I believe the dog's found him, dad!"

"Yes, he's up here. Come along and meet him."

Fred came to the foot of the tree.

"You up there," he said, "come along down."

Not a sound from the tree.

"It's all right," I explained, "he is up there, but he's very
shy. Ask him again."

"All right," said Fred, "Stay there if you want to. But I'm
going to shoot off this gun into the branches just for fun."

And then the man started to come down. As soon as he
touched the ground I jumped up at him.

"This is fine!" I said. "Here's my friend Fred. You'll like
him."

But it wasn't any good. They didn't get along together at

all. They hardly spoke. The man went into the house, and
Fred went after him, carrying his gun. And when they got
into the house it was just the same. The man sat in one chair,
and Fred sat in another, and after a long time some men came
in a motor-car, and the man went away with them. He didn't
say goodbye to me.

When he had gone, Fred and his father made a great fuss of
me. I couldn't understand it. Men are so odd. The man wasn't
a bit pleased that I had brought him and Fred together, but
Fred seemed as if he couldn't do enough for me for having
introduced him to the man. However, Fred's father produced
some cold ham — my favourite dish — and gave me quite a lot
of it, so I stopped worrying over the thing. As mother used to
say, "Don't bother your head about what doesn't concern
you. The only thing a dog need concern himself with is the
bill-of-fare. Eat your bun, and don't make yourself busy about
other people's affairs." Mother's was in some ways a narrow
outlook, but she had a great fund of sterling common sense.

Written by P. G. Wodehouse
Illustrated by Andrew Laws

PASSOVER

Passover is the Jewish festival of
Freedom. In Hebrew, which is the
language of the Jewish people, the
festival is called Pesach. It remembers
the time, many centuries ago, when
the Israelites were released from
being slaves in Egypt. The Pharoah of
the time, thought to have been
Rameses II, only agreed to free the
slaves after God had sent a series of
ten plagues to afflict the Egyptian
people.

The leader of the Israelites was
called Moses and he led his tribe out
of Egypt, across the Red Sea and into
the desert where they wandered for
forty years before finally reaching the
"Promised Land".

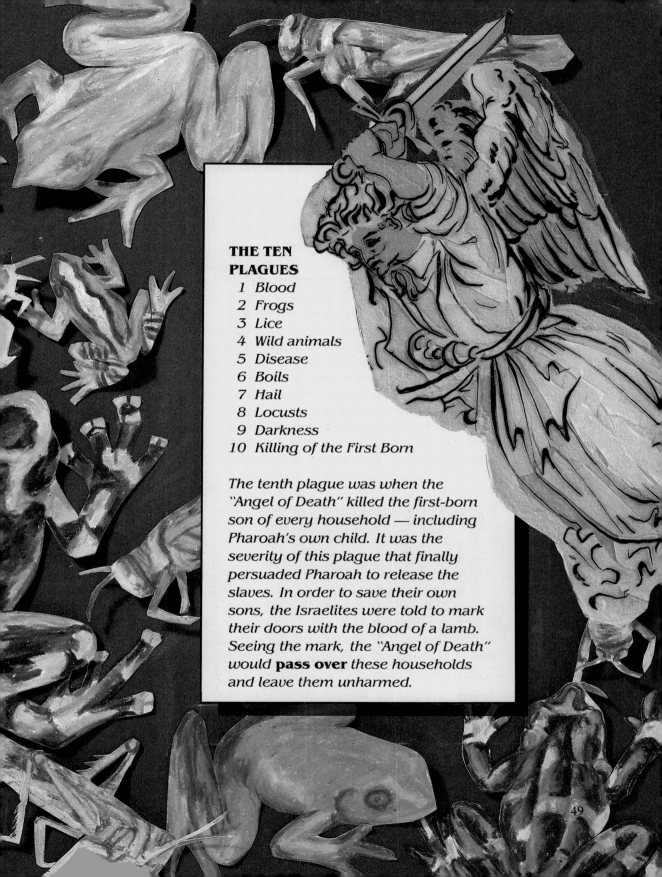

**THE TEN
PLAGUES**

1 *Blood*
2 *Frogs*
3 *Lice*
4 *Wild animals*
5 *Disease*
6 *Boils*
7 *Hail*
8 *Locusts*
9 *Darkness*
10 *Killing of the First Born*

*The tenth plague was when the
"Angel of Death" killed the first-born
son of every household — including
Pharoah's own child. It was the
severity of this plague that finally
persuaded Pharoah to release the
slaves. In order to save their own
sons, the Israelites were told to mark
their doors with the blood of a lamb.
Seeing the mark, the "Angel of Death"
would* **pass over** *these households
and leave them unharmed.*

THE SEDER

During Passover, Jewish families hold a special service in their homes called the Seder. This service consists of songs, prayers and readings and is combined with a festive meal. During the Seder, the story of what happened in Egypt is read from a special book called the Haggadah.

The Seder Plate

Several items are placed on a special **Seder Plate** and referred to during the service.

Baked egg and roasted chicken neck

These represent the festival sacrifices that used to be brought to the Holy Temple in Jerusalem the afternoon before Passover.

Unleavened bread (matzah)*

The Israelites had to leave Egypt in such a hurry that there was no time to wait for their bread to rise.

Salt water*

A reminder of the tears of the slaves.

Bitter herbs*

Symbolic of the bitter suffering of the Israelites in Egypt.

Haroset*

A mixture of chopped apples, walnuts and wine. This mixture is symbolic of the mortar that the slaves used to make bricks from.

Karpas*

A small piece of vegetable, usually parsley, is dipped in the salt water and eaten at the beginning of the Seder as an appetiser and to arouse the curiosity of the children.

The cup of Elijah

A cup of wine put on the table as an invitation to the prophet Elijah, who will announce the coming of the Messiah.

Wine

Four cups of wine are drunk during the Seder as a sign of rejoicing.

The asterisk (*) sign means that this is eaten during the Seder.

Who can beat ATALANTA?

Who was Atalanta?

An amazing young woman, that's who! In one of the Greek myths we are told that Atalanta, the heroine, could outdo the men at hunting, wrestling and running. This was partly because of her upbringing. Disappointed that his child was not a boy, Atalanta's father left her on a hillside to die. Fortunately for Atalanta, animals can be kinder than humans and a passing bear adopted the baby girl, nursed her and kept her warm. She grew into an active, daring child, who was, in time, adopted by some hunters.

Before long, people were talking of this amazing girl who could equal any male hunter. Tales of her adventures grew — she killed two centaurs, the strange half-man, half-horse creatures said to be swifter and stronger than any humans, she helped kill the fierce legendary boar, winning its skin as a reward for her skill, and there was even some talk of her joining the Argonauts in their search for the Golden Fleece.

Her father, hearing about Atalanta, wanted her back as his daughter and tried to make her get married. Atalanta had other ideas. "I'll marry anyone who can beat me in a foot race," she said, and then went back to her hunting and wrestling, secure in the knowledge that no one could. Atalanta was very beautiful so there was an endless stream of athletic young men arriving to race with her. But she always won!

At last Hippomenes arrived. He was fast, but he was also sneaky. He had persuaded Aphrodite, the goddess of love, to give him three golden apples, so beautiful that no one alive could see them and not want them. As soon as Atalanta had begun to outrun him, Hippomenes tossed the first apple so it rolled in front of her. While she stopped to pick it up, he caught up. A moment later he threw the second apple off to the side and while Atalanta swerved to snatch it, Hippomenes got ahead. Atalanta put on a spurt of speed, but just as she surged forward, Hippomenes rolled the third apple off into the grass beside the course. Unable to resist, Atalanta turned aside and her suitor panted across the finishing line.

We are not told if they lived happily ever after, but it is said that they were later turned into lions, which just might have been more fun for Atalanta than settling down to domestic life!

52

THE COUNTRY MAID

An Aesop fable, adapted by *Pat Edwards* and illustrated by *Geoff Hocking.*

One bright day a young milkmaid set off to market with a jug of fine, fresh milk to sell.

BOORA
the first white pelican

Once all pelicans were black. Sleekest and blackest of them all was Boora, the only pelican to own a canoe. He didn't need it of course, not with those big paddling feet of his, but he enjoyed feeling superior to all the other pelicans.

One day after a great storm flooded the river, Boora saw a man and three women trapped on an island in the middle of the surging waters. "Help! Help!" they cried when they saw Boora with his canoe. Boora looked hard at the youngest girl. She was very pretty. "All right," he said, "I'll help," but secretly he was planning to steal the girl for himself.

One by one he ferried them across to dry land, leaving Kantiki, the girl, till last. But Kantiki guessed what he was about, and while he was paddling her older sister across the water, she wrapped the skin rug from her shoulders around a small log of wood. Then she slipped into the water, preferring to risk swimming to safety rather than trusting Boora.

When Boora saw what he thought was the girl asleep, he angrily kicked her and of course, only hurt his foot. Furious over being tricked, he paddled back to his camp. There he splashed himself with white paint the way Aborigines did when about to go off and fight. But before he could set out to capture Kantiki, the older pelicans saw him. Disgusted with the way he looked they drove him from the camp.

However, some of the younger pelicans thought Boora looked rather dashing, so they decided to paint themselves white too. They didn't do a perfect job and that's why today most pelicans are black and white.

An Aboriginal story retold and illustrated by Pat Edwards.

Prince Rabbit

Once upon a time there was a King who had no children. Sometimes he would say to the Queen, "If only we had a son!" and the Queen would answer, "If only we had!" Another day he would say, "If only we had a daughter!" and the Queen would sigh and answer, "Yes, even if we had a daughter, that would be something". But they had no children at all.

As the years went on, and there were still no children in the Royal palace, the people began to ask each other who would be the next King to reign over them. And some said that perhaps it would be the Chancellor, which was a pity, as nobody liked him very much; and others said that there would be no King at all, but that everybody would be equal. Those who were lowest of all thought that this would be a satisfactory ending of the matter, but those who were higher up felt that, though in some respects it would be a good thing, yet in other respects it would be an ill-advised state of affairs; and they hoped, therefore, that a young Prince would be born in the palace. But no Prince was born.

One day, when the Chancellor was in audience with the King, it seemed well to him to speak what was in the people's minds.

"Your Majesty," he said, and then stopped, wondering how best to put it.

"Well?" said the King.

"Have I Your Majesty's permission to speak my mind?"

"So far, yes," said the King.

Encouraged by this, the Chancellor resolved to put the matter plainly. "In the event of Your Majesty's death —" He coughed and began again. "If Your Majesty ever *should* die," he said, "which in any case will not be for many years — if ever — as, I need hardly say, Your Majesty's loyal subjects earnestly hope — I mean they hope it will be never. But assuming for the moment — making the sad assumption —"

"You said you wanted to speak your mind," interrupted the King. "Is that it?"

"Yes, Majesty."

"Then I don't think much of it."

"Thank you, Your Majesty."

"What you are trying to say is, 'Who will be the next King?'"

"Quite so, Your Majesty."

"Ah!" The King was silent for a little. Then he said, "I can tell you who won't be".

The Chancellor did not seek for information on this point, feeling that in the circumstances the answer was obvious.

"What do you suggest yourself?"

"That Your Majesty choose a successor from among the young and the highly born of this country, putting him to whatever test seems good to Your Majesty."

The King pulled at his beard and frowned. "There must be not one test, but many tests. Let all who will offer themselves, provided only they are under the age of twenty and well born. See to it."

He waved his hand in dismissal, and with an accuracy established by long practice, the Chancellor retired backwards out of the palace.

On the following morning, therefore, it was announced that all those who were ambitious to be appointed the King's successor, and who were of high birth and not yet come to the age of twenty, should present themselves a week later for the tests to which His Majesty desired to put them, the first of which would be a running race. Whereat the people rejoiced, for they wished to be ruled by one to whom they could look up, and running was much esteemed in that country.

On the appointed day the excitement was great. All along the course, which was once round the castle, large crowds were massed, and at the finishing point the King and Queen themselves were seated in a specially erected pavilion. And to this the competitors were brought to be introduced to Their Majesties. There were nine young nobles, well built and handsome and (it was thought) intelligent, who were competitors. And there was also one Rabbit.

The Chancellor had first noticed the Rabbit when he was lining up the competitors, pinning numbers on their backs so that the people should identify them, and giving them such instructions as seemed necessary to him. "Now, now, be off with you," he said. "Competitors only, this way." And he made a motion of impatient dismissal with his foot.

"I *am* a competitor," said the Rabbit. "And I don't think it is usual," he added with dignity, "for the starter to kick one of the competitors just at the beginning of an important foot race. It looks like favouritism."

"*You* can't be a competitor," laughed all the nobles.

"Why not? Read the rules."

The Chancellor, feeling rather hot suddenly, read the rules. The Rabbit was certainly under twenty; he had a pedigree which showed that he was of the highest birth; and —

"And," said the Rabbit, "I am ambitious to be appointed the King's successor. Those were all the conditions. Now let's get on with the race."

But first came the introduction to the King. One by one the competitors came up . . . and at the end —

"This," said the Chancellor, as airily as he could, "is Rabbit".

Rabbit bowed in the most graceful manner possible, first to the King and then to the Queen. But the King only stared at him. Then he turned to the Chancellor.

"Well?"

The Chancellor shrugged his shoulders. "His entry does not appear to lack validity," he said.

"He means, Your Majesty, that it is all right," explained Rabbit.

The King laughed suddenly. "Go on," he said. "We can always have a race for a new Chancellor afterwards."

So the race was started. And the young Lord Calomel was much cheered on coming in second, not only by Their Majesties, but also by Rabbit, who had finished the course some time before and was now lounging in the Royal pavilion.

"A very good style, Your Majesty," said Rabbit, turning to the King. "Altogether he seems to be a most promising youth."

"Most," said the King grimly. "So much so that I do not propose to trouble the rest of the competitors. The next test shall take place between you and him."

"Not racing again, please, Your Majesty. That would hardly be fair to His Lordship."

"No, not racing. Fighting."

"Ah! What sort of fighting?"

"With swords," said the King.

"I am a little rusty with swords, but I daresay in a day or two —"

"It will be now," said the King.

"You mean, Your Majesty, as soon as Lord Calomel has recovered his breath?"

The King answered nothing, but turned to his Chancellor. "Tell the young Lord Calomel that in half an hour I desire him to fight with this Rabbit —"

"The young Lord Rabbit," murmured the other competitor to the Chancellor.

"To fight with him for my kingdom."

"*And* borrow me a sword, will you?" said Rabbit. "Quite a small one. I don't want to hurt him."

So, half an hour later, on a level patch of grass in front of the pavilion, the fight began. It was a short but exciting struggle. Calomel, whirling his long sword in his strong right arm, dashed upon Rabbit, and Rabbit, carrying his short sword in his teeth, dodged between Calomel's legs and brought him toppling. And when it was seen that the young lord rose from the ground with a broken arm, and that with the utmost gallantry he had now taken his sword in his left hand, the people cheered. And Rabbit, dropping his sword for a moment, cheered too, and then he picked it up and got it entangled in his adversary's legs again, so that again young Lord Calomel crashed to the ground, this time with a sprained ankle. And so there he lay.

Rabbit trotted into the Royal pavilion and dropped his sword in the Chancellor's lap.

66

"Thank you so much," he said. "Have I won?" And the King frowned and pulled at his beard. "There are other tests," he muttered.

But what were they to be? It was plain that Lord Calomel was in no condition for another physical test. What, then, of an intellectual test?

"After all," said the King to the Queen that night, "intelligence is a quality not without value in a ruler".

"Is it?" asked the Queen doubtfully.

"I have found it so," said the King, a trifle haughtily.

"Oh," said the Queen.

"There is a riddle of which my father was fond, the answer to which has never been revealed save to the Royal House. We might make this the final test between them."

"What is the riddle?"

"I fancy it goes like this." He thought for a moment and then recited it, beating time with his hand.

"My first I *do for your daylight*,
Although 'tis neither black nor white.
My second looks the other way,
Yet always goes to bed by day.
My whole can fly and climb a tree,
And sometimes swims upon the sea."

"What is the answer?" asked the Queen.

"As far as I remember," said His Majesty, "it is either *Dormouse* or *Raspberry*".

"*Dormouse* doesn't make sense," objected the Queen.

"Neither does *Raspberry*," pointed out the King.

"Then how can they guess it?"

"They can't. But my idea is that young Calomel should be secretly told

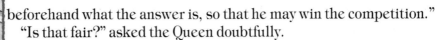beforehand what the answer is, so that he may win the competition."

"Is that fair?" asked the Queen doubtfully.

"Yes," said the King. "Certainly. Or I wouldn't have suggested it."

So it was duly announced by the Chancellor that the final test between the young Lord Calomel and Rabbit would be the solving of an ancient riddle-me-ree which in the past had baffled all save those of Royal blood. Copies of the riddle had been sent to the competitors, and in a week from that day they would be called upon to give their answers before Their Majesties and the full court. And with Lord Calomel's copy went a message, which said this:

"*From a Friend.* The answer is *Dormouse.* **Burn this.**"

The day came around; and Calomel and Rabbit were brought before Their Majesties; and they bowed to Their Majesties and were ordered to be seated, for Calomel's ankle was still painful to him. And when the Chancellor had called for silence, the King addressed those present, explaining the conditions of the test to them.

"And the answer to the riddle," he said, "is in this sealed paper, which I now hand to my Chancellor, in order that he shall open it as soon as the competitors have told us what they know of the matter".

The people, being uncertain what else to do, cheered slightly.

"I will ask Lord Calomel first," His Majesty went on. He looked at His Lordship, and His Lordship nodded slightly. And Rabbit, noticing that nod, smiled suddenly to himself.

The young Lord Calomel tried to look very wise, and he said, "There are many

possible answers to this riddle-me-ree, but the best answer seems to me to be *Dormouse*".

"Let someone take a note of that answer," said the King: whereupon the chief secretary wrote down: **Lord Calomel —** *Dormouse*.

"Now," said the King to Rabbit, "what suggestion have you to make in this matter?"

Rabbit, who had spent an anxious week inventing answers each more impossible than the last, looked down modestly.

"Well?" said the King.

"Your Majesty," said the Rabbit with some apparent hesitation, "I have a great respect for the intelligence of the young Lord Calomel, but I think in this matter he is mistaken. The answer is not, as he suggests, *Wood-louse*, but *Dormouse*."

"I said *Dormouse*," cried Calomel indignantly.

"I thought you said *Wood-louse*," said Rabbit in surprise.

"He certainly said *Dormouse*," said the King coldly.

"*Wood-louse*, I think," said Rabbit.

"**Lord Calomel —** *Dormouse*," read out the chief secretary.

"There you are," said Calomel, "I did say *Dormouse*."

"My apologies," said Rabbit, with a bow. "Then we are both right, for *Dormouse* it certainly is."

The Chancellor broke open the sealed paper and, to the amazement of nearly all present, read out, "*Dormouse* . . . Apparently, Your Majesty," he said in some surprise, "they are both equally correct".

The King scowled. In some way which he didn't quite understand, he had been tricked.

69

"May I suggest, Your Majesty," the Chancellor went on, "that they be asked now some question of a different order, such as can be answered, after not more than a few minutes thought, here in Your Majesty's presence? Some problem in the higher mathematics, for instance, such as might be profitable for a future King to know."

"What question?" asked His Majesty, a little nervously.

"Well, as an example — what is seven times six?" And behind his hand he whispered to the King, "Forty-two".

Not a muscle of the King's face moved, but he looked thoughtfully at the Lord Calomel. Supposing His Lordship did not know!

"Well?" he said reluctantly. "What is the answer?"

The young Lord Calomel thought for some time and then said, "Fifty-four".

"And you?" said the King to Rabbit.

Rabbit wondered what to say. As long as he gave the same answers as Calomel, he could not lose in the encounter, yet in this case, "forty-two" was the right answer. But the King, who could do no wrong, even in arithmetic, might decide, for the purposes of the competition, that "fifty-four" was an answer more becoming to the future ruler of the country. Was it, then, safe to say "forty-two"?

"Your Majesty," he said, "there are several possible answers to this extraordinary novel conundrum. At first sight the obvious solution would appear to be "forty-two". The objection to this solution is that it lacks originality. I have long felt that a progressive country such as ours might well strike out a new line in the matter. Let us agree that in future seven sixes are fifty-four. In that case the answer, as Lord Calomel has pointed out, is 'fifty-four'. But if Your Majesty would prefer to cling to the old style of counting, then Your Majesty and Your Majesty's Chancellor would make the answer 'forty-two'."

After saying which, Rabbit bowed gracefully, both to Their Majesties and to his opponent, and sat down again.

The King scratched his head in a puzzled sort of way. "The correct answer," he said, "is, or will be in future, 'fifty-four'".

"Make a note of that," whispered the Chancellor to the chief secretary.

"Lord Calomel guessed this at his first attempt; Rabbit at his second attempt. I therefore declare Lord Calomel the winner."

"Shame!" said Rabbit.

"Who said that?" cried the King furiously.

Rabbit looked over his shoulder with the object of identifying the culprit, but was apparently unsuccessful.

"However," went on the King, "in order that there should be no doubts in the minds of my people as to the absolute fairness with which this competition is being conducted, there will be one further test. It happens that a King is often called upon to make speeches and exhortations to his people, and for this purpose ability to stand evenly upon two legs for a considerable length of time is of much value to him. The next test, therefore, will be —"

But at this point Lord Calomel suddenly cleared his throat so loudly that the King had perforce to stop and listen to him.

"Quite so," said the King. "The next test, therefore, will be held in a month's time, when His Lordship's ankle is healed, and it will be a test to see who can balance himself longest upon two legs only."

Rabbit lolloped back to his home in the wood, pondering deeply.

Now, there was an enchanter who lived in the wood, a man of many magical gifts. He could (it was averred by the countryside) extract coloured ribbons from his mouth, cook plum puddings in a hat, and produce as many as ten handkerchiefs, knotted together, from a twist of paper. And that night, after a simple dinner of salad, Rabbit called upon him.

"Can you," he said, "turn a rabbit into a man?"

The enchanter considered this carefully. "I can," he said at last, "turn a plum pudding into a rabbit."

"That," said Rabbit, "to be frank, would not be a helpful operation".

"I can turn almost anything into a rabbit," said the enchanter with growing enthusiasm. "In fact, I like doing it."

Then Rabbit had an idea. "Can you turn a man into a rabbit?"

"I did once. At least, I turned a baby into a baby rabbit."

"When was that?"

"Eighteen years ago. At the court of King Nicodemus. I was giving an exhibition of my powers to him and his good Queen. I asked one of the company to lend me a baby, never thinking for a moment that — The young Prince was handed up. I put a red silk handkerchief over him and waved my hands. Then I took the handkerchief away . . . The Queen was very distressed. I tried everything I could, but it was useless. The King was most generous about it. He said that I could keep the rabbit. I carried it about with me for some weeks, but one day it escaped. Dear, dear!" He wiped his eyes gently with a red silk handkerchief.

"Most interesting," said Rabbit. "Well, this is what I want you to do." And they discussed the matter from the beginning.

A month later the great standing competition was to take place. When all was ready, the King rose to make his opening remarks.

"We are now," he began, "to make one of the most interesting tests between our two candidates for the throne. At the word 'Go!' they will —" and then he stopped suddenly. "Why, what's this?" he said, putting on his spectacles. "Where is the young Lord Calomel? And what is that second rabbit doing? There was no need to bring your brother," he added severely to Rabbit.

"I am Lord Calomel," said the second rabbit meekly.

"Oh!" said the King.

"Go!" said the Chancellor, who was a little deaf.

Rabbit, who had been practising for a month, jumped on his back paws and remained there. Lord Calomel, who had had no practice at all, remained on all fours. In the crowd at the back the enchanter chuckled to himself.

"How long do I stay like this?" asked Rabbit.

"This is all very awkward and distressing," said the King.

"May I get down?" said Rabbit.

"There is no doubt that Rabbit has won," said the Chancellor.

"Which rabbit?" cried the King crossly. "They're both rabbits."

"The one with the white spots behind the ears," said Rabbit helpfully. "May I get down?"

There was a sudden cry from the back of the hall. "Your Majesty?"

"Well, well, what is it?"

The enchanter pushed his way forward. "May I look, Your Majesty?" he said in a trembling voice. "White spots behind the ears? Dear, dear! Allow me!" He seized Rabbit's ears and bent them this way and that.

"Ow!" said Rabbit.

"It is! Your Majesty, it is!"

"Is what?"

"The son of the late King Nicodemus, whose country is now joined to your own. Prince Silvio."

"Quite so," said Rabbit airily, hiding his surprise. "Didn't any of you recognise me?"

"Nicodemus only had one son," said the Chancellor, "and he died as a baby".

"Not died," said the enchanter, and forthwith explained the whole sad story.

"I see," said the King, when the story was ended. "But of course that is neither here nor there. A competition like this must be conducted with absolute impartiality. "He turned to the Chancellor. "Which of them won that last test?"

"Prince Silvio," said the Chancellor.

"Then, my dear Prince Silvio —"

"One moment," interrupted the enchanter excitedly. "I've just thought of the words. I *knew* there were some words you had to say."

He threw back his red silk hankerchief over Rabbit and cried, "Hey presto!"

And the handkerchief rose and rose and rose . . . And there was Prince Silvio!

You can imagine how loudly the people cheered. But the King appeared not to notice that anything surprising had happened.

"Then, my dear Prince Silvio," he went on, "as the winner of this most interesting series of contests, you are appointed successor to our throne".

"Your Majesty," said Silvio, "this is too much". And he turned to the enchanter and said, "May I borrow your handkerchief for a moment? My emotion has overcome me."

So on the following day Prince Rabbit was duly proclaimed heir to the throne before all the people. But not until the ceremony was over did he return the enchanter's red handkerchief.

"And now," he said to the enchanter, "you may restore Lord Calomel to his proper shape".

And the enchanter placed his handkerchief on Lord Calomel's head and said, "Hey presto!" and Lord Calomel stretched himself and said, "Thanks very much". But he said it rather coldly, as if he were not really very grateful.

So they all lived happily for a long time. And Prince Rabbit married the most beautiful Princess of those parts, and when a son was born to them there was much feasting and jollification. And the King gave a great party, whereat minstrels, tumblers, jugglers and suchlike were present in large quantities to give pleasure to the company. But, in spite of a suggestion made by the Princess, the enchanter was not present.

"But I hear he is so clever," said the Princess to her husband.

"He has many amusing inventions," replied the Prince, "but some of them are not in the best of taste".

"Very well, dear," said the Princess.

Written by A. A. Milne
Illustrated by Azoo

75

MY BROTHER GETS LETTERS

My brother gets letters — not many, but some,
I don't know why — but I get none.
Odd people seem to write to him —
a card to say his bike's done or a library book's in.
He seems to have friends, who when they're away
write about their holiday,
like — "We're near the beach, — had chips last night,
my bed squeaks and sand fleas bite."
And sometimes he gets letters out of the blue
from people who can't know who they're writing to
offering him *The Reader's Digest Bird Book* cheap
or adverts for films like "The Blobs" —
GIANT JELLIES THAT EAT AS THEY CREEP.
But I don't get anything. No one writes to me.
That is — until just recently.

You see I was looking at the paper one day
and I was reading about this man's brain — it was
    fading away.
That is — until he had done this "Memory Course"
and discovered his Inner Mind Force.
And when you got down to the end
It said: "This sounds **GREAT** — please send
to me at this address now:
**"SO YOU WANT TO SAVE BRAIN-CELLS? —
    HERE'S HOW".**
And you filled in your name and address along
    dotted lines
and sent it off to: "Great Minds
    P.O. Box 16, Manchester 8."
It was as simple as that. Sit and wait.
Now as it happens I wasn't very worried about my
    Inner Mind Force
or the ones to cure baldness or put me on a
    slimming course,
but the thing was — they all had something for free
which they promised they'd send — addressed to me.
What could be better?
I'd get a letter.
So after I'd got some of these forms together
I came back then to my brother
and I said: "I bet, out of us two,
I get more letters than you".
And he said: "Rubbish, no-one ever writes to you,
you're a Nobody, a No-one-knows-who".

"Right," I said, "we'll keep a score,
me and you — see who gets more".
"Great," he said, and shook my hand. "Done!
What do I get," he said, "when I've won?"
"No prizes," I said. "But whoever loses,
will have to do whatever the winner chooses."
"Great," he said again — and laughed,
he must have thought I was daft
to take him on.
He thought he couldn't go wrong.
"I'll show him," I thought. "What I can't wait to see
is his face when these people write back to me."

So anyway, I sent off about three or four
and soon I got what I was hoping for.
A former Mr Universe had written to say:
"BUILD POWER-PACKED MUSCLES
in just 70 seconds a day!!!"
"There you are," I said to my brother.
"A letter — one nil — and tomorrow I'll be getting another."
So while he read what they had sent me
"Rippling muscles on guarantee
see your strength rise
right before your very eyes
on the built-in **POWER-METER**,"
I sat tight for my next letter.

Next to come through the post was Harvey Speke.
"I see my years of fatness as a past nightmare I'll
      never repeat.
Why be fat when you can be slim?
Shrink your waistline, stomach and chin,
I used to look like **THIS** — believe it or not!"
And there were pictures of bellies and heaven knows what
before and after shrinking with the Miracle Pill.
I didn't read the rest — "Two nil!"
I said to my brother. "I'm winning, aren't I?
You can't win now." But he says: "Oh can't I?"
and I can see he's getting really angry
reading about pills to stop you feeling hungry.

Next day there were two more —
one was a rather glossy brochure
on an Old Age Pension Plan
and the other on Shoes For The Larger Man.
For three days he hadn't got anything through the post.
He sat there at breakfast munching his toast
staring at his plate while I was making a neat stack
of leaflets and letters I'd got back.
"Four nil now, isn't it? Give in?
You see," I said, "every day I'm getting something".
And sure enough *something* arrived not long after
but it wasn't quite what *I* was after.

It was a great big parcel — it had come from Liverpool.
"Who's it for?" I said. "You, you fool."
It was the first parcel I'd ever had in my life.
"Go on — open it," father said, "here's a knife".
And they all stood round to see who'd sent a parcel to me.
Even my brother wanted to see.
It was wrapped in red paper but the box was brown.
I pulled the lid off — and it was an eiderdown.
It was what is nowadays called a Quilt for a bed,
But we used to call them "eiderdowns", instead.
"What is it?" "A pillow?"
"Who sent it?" "I don't know."
"How much did it cost you?" "What do you mean?"
"Don't be funny — he hasn't got a bean."
I panicked. I came over cold.
Don't forget — I was only nine years old.

"Did you send off for this thing?"
"No," I said. "All I did was fill a form thing in,
it said there was something for free —
fill in the form and it'd come to me."
"Fat-head! That means free till the seventh day,
keep it longer than that and you've got to pay.
Send it back if you don't.
Mind you — I bet you won't."
"Don't say that," said mother, "he wasn't to know better".
"But what was he doing?" "I wanted a letter."
"Well get your friend Mart to send you cards from
    Wales when he goes
instead of sending off for boxes of bed-clothes."
I felt such an idiot looking at the eiderdown.
I looked at my brother. He looked round.
"What's the matter? Five nil. Well done."
He laughed. "I think you've won
or do you want to go on for a bit more?"
"No no no," I said, "I don't care about the score".
"So you'll wrap up the box and send it back?" father said.
"Unless you want to pay for a new eiderdown on your bed."
But I didn't do it straightaway,
and I didn't do it the next day,
or the next, or the next,
the eiderdown and the wrapping were in a gigantic mess.
"The eiderdown's growing." I was thinking,
"No! The box to send it back in's shrinking."

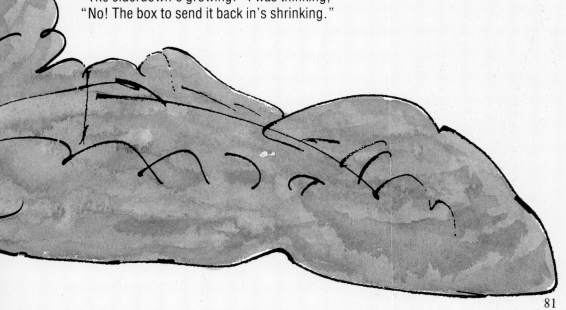

Anyway fourth day on — eiderdown still not sent
we were all having tea — the doorbell went.
My brother looks up. "Probably the police —
on the hunt for an eiderdown thief."
Father went to see who was there
and we could hear voices from where we were.
Moment later — he's back — very long in the face,
he looks at me. "It's for you," he says.
I could have died. "Is it the police
on the hunt for an eiderdown thief?"
"No," he says, "there's a man out there.
He's got something for you." "Out where?
Men don't come round here for me."
But I went to the door and they all followed to see.
"Mr Rosen, is it?" The man looked.
He was reading my name out of a black book.
"No," I said. "You want my father."
"*M.* Rosen?" he says. "He's *H,* I gather."
I said, "Yes. I'm M."
So he says, "Good. Right then,
it's outside. Shall I wheel it in?"
"What?" I said. "The washing machine."
"Washing machine? Oh no. Not for me."
"Well it says here '*M.* Rosen', all right. Do you want to see?"
"No," I said, "I only send for free things".
"Yes, the demonstrations *are* free," he says, "but not
    the washing machines".
"I don't want it." I looked round for help.
You can imagine how I felt.
But they were hiding behind the door
laughing their heads off — my brother on the floor.
I turned back. Looked up at the man.
"I've brought it now," he says. "It's in the van."
"I've come all the way from Hoover's to show it you."
"No," I said. "No?" he said. "Haven't you got anyone
    else I could show it to?"
For a moment — it felt like a week —
he looked down at me — I looked down at my feet.
Then he shut his book and went, and I shut the door,
and straightaway my brother was there with "Shall I
    add that to your score?"

Six nil? Have you won yet?"
I said, "I've had enough of this letter bet".
And he said, "Why? Don't you want a washing machine?
You could use it to keep your eiderdown clean!"
"Oh no! The eiderdown." For a moment I'd
    forgotten about it.
"I can't get it in. The box: — it's shrunk!" I shouted.
But mum said, "I'll help you send that back, don't worry,
but what's coming next? A coat? A lorry?"
But father said, "Who's won this bet?
And what's the winner going to get?"
My brother looked really happy and said, "I've lost —
Letters? *He's* the one that gets the most."
"All I want," I said, "is I don't want to hear any
    more about it.
If I have to send off to get a letter — I'm better off
    without it."
"OK," my brother said, "let's call it square".
"Yes," I said, "we'll leave it there".

But even now —
when there's someone asking for me at the door,
who mum has never seen before,
she says to me: "It's for you, dear.
Quick! Your eiderdown's here!"

Written by Michael Rosen
Illustrated by Quentin Blake

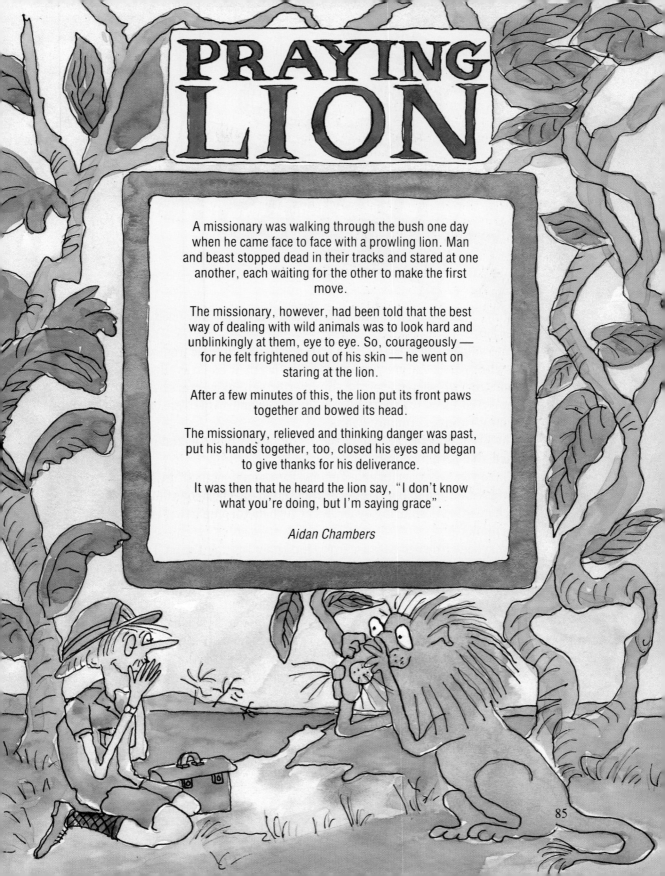

PRAYING LION

A missionary was walking through the bush one day when he came face to face with a prowling lion. Man and beast stopped dead in their tracks and stared at one another, each waiting for the other to make the first move.

The missionary, however, had been told that the best way of dealing with wild animals was to look hard and unblinkingly at them, eye to eye. So, courageously — for he felt frightened out of his skin — he went on staring at the lion.

After a few minutes of this, the lion put its front paws together and bowed its head.

The missionary, relieved and thinking danger was past, put his hands together, too, closed his eyes and began to give thanks for his deliverance.

It was then that he heard the lion say, "I don't know what you're doing, but I'm saying grace".

Aidan Chambers

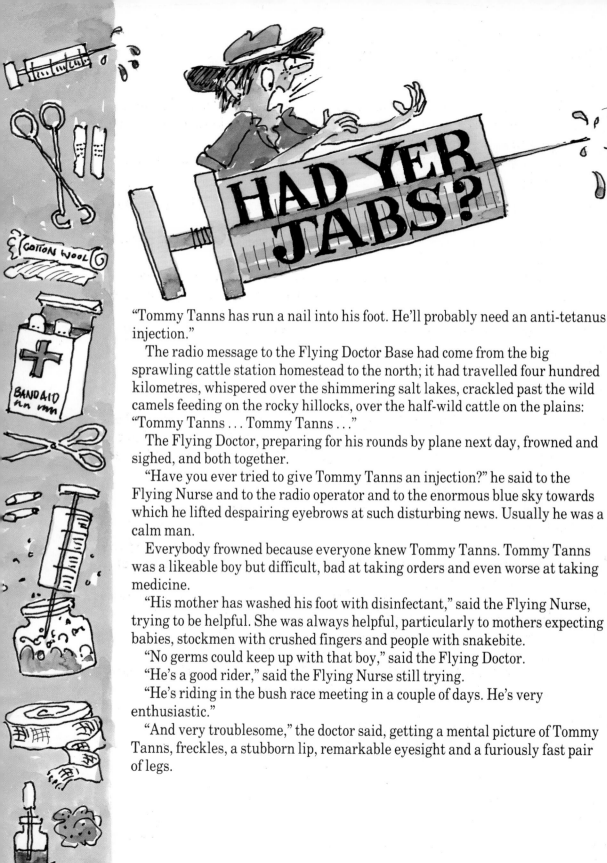

HAD YER JABS?

"Tommy Tanns has run a nail into his foot. He'll probably need an anti-tetanus injection."

The radio message to the Flying Doctor Base had come from the big sprawling cattle station homestead to the north; it had travelled four hundred kilometres, whispered over the shimmering salt lakes, crackled past the wild camels feeding on the rocky hillocks, over the half-wild cattle on the plains: "Tommy Tanns ... Tommy Tanns ..."

The Flying Doctor, preparing for his rounds by plane next day, frowned and sighed, and both together.

"Have you ever tried to give Tommy Tanns an injection?" he said to the Flying Nurse and to the radio operator and to the enormous blue sky towards which he lifted despairing eyebrows at such disturbing news. Usually he was a calm man.

Everybody frowned because everyone knew Tommy Tanns. Tommy Tanns was a likeable boy but difficult, bad at taking orders and even worse at taking medicine.

"His mother has washed his foot with disinfectant," said the Flying Nurse, trying to be helpful. She was always helpful, particularly to mothers expecting babies, stockmen with crushed fingers and people with snakebite.

"No germs could keep up with that boy," said the Flying Doctor.

"He's a good rider," said the Flying Nurse still trying.

"He's riding in the bush race meeting in a couple of days. He's very enthusiastic."

"And very troublesome," the doctor said, getting a mental picture of Tommy Tanns, freckles, a stubborn lip, remarkable eyesight and a furiously fast pair of legs.

There were other children to see tomorrow, throats to be examined, eyes to be looked at, pulses to be taken, tongues to be poked out, injections to give. It was routine.

All except ten-year-old Tommy Tanns. Whatever else Tommy was, he was never routine.

"You're going to have an anti-tetanus shot today," said Angela, and then she knew she shouldn't have told her brother.

"WHAT?" he yelled scrambling for the door. "I'm NOT. I'm not going to be jabbed with that needle, I'm not."

Then he was out into the wide dusty yard of the station homestead and heading for the horse yard with Angela, who had screamed for help, Marie, the Aboriginal girl who helped in the house, and his mother after him.

He ran faster than the lot of them, despite his sore foot, his muscular sunburned legs working like pistons.

"You silly boy," his mother yelled. "You have to have the injection."

"You're a coward!" screamed Angela. "You're a great fat coward."

At this moment Bill Owen, a stockman, came up.

Mrs Tanns said: "Bill, catch Tommy for us. The Flying Doctor is due, and the children are coming from the out-stations, as well as the Aboriginal children from the camp. Tommy has to have an injection. And look at him. Just look at him."

"Mum!" screamed Angela. "He's got a horse!"

Tommy had caught a horse, put on the bridle and was galloping on it barebacked out the gate.

Bill Owen looked around for another horse but he knew it wasn't much good. Tommy could ride like a demon and would be off into some difficult corner of the low, rocky hills nearby.

Meanwhile a car had entered the yard. It had a group of chastened children sitting in a grumpy row with Mrs Hills from the out-station driving.

"Here we are," she called. "All happy and gay for our medicals and our needles. What's up?"

"Tommy," said Mrs Tanns, "has just run off again. Angela told him he was going to have his anti-tetanus. Angela, I wish you'd hold your tongue sometimes."

"He's run off AGAIN," said Mrs Hills.

"Yes again. I don't know what the doctor will say."

The Flying Doctor looked from his aircraft as the pilot made his usual careful approach to the station strip and said suddenly: "There's a horseman going lick for leather."

He looked again and sighed deeply as the plane came in low to touch down with a spurt and whirl of dust behind, past the fat, languid, brown sausage of the windsock that lifted and drooped in the gritty breeze.

"I might have known. It's young Tommy running off again. He has to have an anti-tetanus shot. We'll have to do something about that boy."

"Well, get them to yard him, tie his legs and keep him locked up until you come."

The pilot, Jack, was a laconic type. He had children of his own, and there was no funny business with them! All disciplined. Even his aeroplane behaved itself.

"Maybe," he said, "you'd like me to try some low flying while you lasso him from the plane?"

"Well," said the doctor, "at least the rest of them are here".

For the next half hour or so throats were examined, pulses taken, arms dabbed and injections given amid some tears, screwed-up faces, determined I-won't-cry-if-it-kills-me looks and the doctor's, "There it didn't hurt, did it?"

Apart from some anguish there was also general resentment.

"Why," said one small girl, "do we have to have jabs when Tommy doesn't? It's not fair".

"It's not fair to me either," said the doctor, looking around at the circle of small, stern faces and feeling mean and inadequate.

Jack, the pilot, didn't help.

"Why don't you parachute and land on top of him, Doc?" he said.

Mrs Tanns looked dismayed. "Doctor, I'm sorry he's slipped through our fingers again."

Suddenly the doctor had a thought. It seemed a good one.

He checked with the pilot, "How are we off for fuel and time?"

Tommy watched from a nearby stony hill until the plane took off. He could see the Flying Doctor in it. He watched it swing off in a wide circle and he dug his bare feet into the horse and trotted back to the station.

His mother appeared vexed, and the rest of the children scowled at him.

"Had yer jabs?" he asked casually.

The scowls deepened.

"Don't come near us," said Angela. "You're full of germs, the doctor said."

The other children stuck their heads in the air.

"Come inside, Tommy," said his mother wearily. "Come inside." She got him into the room and brought a frosted jug of cordial from the refrigerator.

"You're thirsty after your ride, I suppose."

"Yes, Mum."

"I wish you wouldn't run away like that."

"Yes, Mum."

A shadow fell across the big wire-screened door. Bill Owen was standing outside rolling a cigarette casually.

"What's he doin' there?" asked the boy suspiciously.

"He's having a bit of a spell, I suppose."

Tommy thought about it. Bill Owen wasn't the sort who took a spell at that time of day.

"More cordial, Tommy?"

He looked at her suspiciously. Something was up. She set the glass jug beside him, her best jug with little beads of moisture running down its sides. The boy poured himself another glass. Then he heard it. It was the beat of a plane's engine, and there was something distinctive about it.

The Flying Doctor was coming back.

"COMING BACK."

Tommy shouted it aloud and was on his feet in an instant.

"Now you sit down," said Mrs Tanns determinedly. "You stay where you are."

"Yes," said Bill Owen, unwisely opening the door. "Just stay where you are."

The plane came roaring over the station as it headed for its landing.

Suddenly the boy shouted, "CATCH, BILL".

90

Bill Owen saw that good jug in mid air spilling cordial coming straight at him. He caught the jug but the boy went past at the same time, twisting and turning.

Tommy grabbed a stockwhip as he ran from the verandah and cracked it threateningly at the group of girls who ran to intercept.

Jack, the pilot, had taxied his plane nearly to the station, and the prop had hardly stopped swinging before the doctor and pilot were out after Tommy.

But Tommy had a good start. He'd worked out his plan. His retreat to the horse yard was cut off so he headed for the windmill with its high tower and went up the ladder like a monkey.

And there he stayed just below the windmill stand, hanging on with one arm (and legs) with the whip ready in the other.

"First one up gets a crack."

"Be reasonable, Tommy. You're wasting time. It's for your own good, boy," the Flying Doctor pleaded. It would have been more sense talking to the crows that sat cawing on a nearby fence.

"Let me get at him," said Jack, the pilot, and he began climbing the ladder. You wouldn't find his kids behaving like this. Jack believed in discipline. Kids needed firm handling.

"Now you come down, Tommy, or you'll get a thrashing."

"And you come up and YOU'LL get a thrashing," the boy yelled.

He waited until the pilot was nearly in range and then cracked the whip over his head. Jack, the pilot, ducked and went down the ladder again. This infuriated all the children who were watching below although it seemed to amuse the crows.

"The young devil's dangerous," Jack said. "He's uncontrollable."

"Any more ideas?" The Flying Doctor looked amused.

"Your idea of flying off and then coming back wasn't too good either, Doc," said the pilot. He felt he'd lost face, and certainly he'd nearly lost some of it from that whipcracker up in the windmills.

"Well," said the pilot, looking at his watch, "we've a schedule to keep. We'll have to try another day, Doc."

"Mrs Tanns, Tommy's riding in the bush races in a couple of days, isn't he?"

Mrs Tanns nodded, "He wouldn't miss them. A few people even think he'll win. A few people do...."

"Do they?" said the doctor thoughtfully.

Up the windmill, Tommy saw the Flying Doctor's plane take off.

"Missed again, Doctor," he shouted, and didn't care who heard.

To Angela's disappointment Tommy didn't get tetanus, while other people who'd had inoculations for various other things suffered and had sore arms.

"Had yer jabs?" Tommy would say scornfully, but mostly he was training his own horse Wallaby, doing sprints around the horse paddock while Jack Longa, the Aboriginal stockman, gave him starting practice.

"Ol' Wallaby will have to go faster than that, Tommy," said Jack Longa. "The other horses will eat 'im."

Tommy knew it in his heart. Wallaby was a slow starter and Angela came to taunt him through the fence.

"Slow coach. Slow coach."

He galloped the horse past her kicking up grit in her face.

"Had yer jabs?" he asked unpleasantly.

The race-track was in a dusty stretch of saltbush, a dirt track circling it with rough and ready rails. It was a fine inland day, the sky a hard blue, a wedge-tail eagle riding the warm thermals with a slow easy majesty, its sharp eye taking in the movement and tumult below.

The area around the finishing post was alive with people. A number of planes were parked in the small bush strip nearby, with more cars arriving trailing banners of dust. The dust was everywhere and even on the race programme — for the main race was the Duststorm Derby.

The starter was a man who stood in front of the horses, just inside the rail, and dropped his hat as a signal. It was all very informal, and there were plenty of drinks and coppers full of boiling water for tea in the brushwood tea room. The hotel bar stood under a galvanised iron roof, and propped against it, for it was nothing more than a lot of tables, were stockmen and rouseabouts, station owners and other fanciers of horse flesh. The women wore their best dresses. The race secretary hurried to and fro from his little iron shed. The course announcer stood in the back of the truck and used a microphone and public address system that screamed and groaned and crackled. It mightn't have been the Melbourne Cup, but it was a big day outback.

Tommy knew it was time to change into his silks for the big race. His mother had made them. And he was proud of them as he was of Wallaby, although Wallaby had him worried a bit. That slow start....

For a moment he was off his guard and people suddenly converged on him. First there was the Flying Nurse with a bottle and some cotton wool. Then Bill Owen, Jack Longa, his mother, Angela and, horror of horrors, the Flying Doctor appeared with a syringe.

"Now!" shouted the doctor.

They all grabbed him. He struggled and kicked.

"Hold his arm. Hold his arm."

But the arm flailed to and fro, and he wriggled and fought until his bottom part was in the air and his arms were down in the dust.

"The bottom will do," said the doctor. "Quick, Nurse." The Flying Nurse was ready. She gave a wipe of bare skin with the cotton wool; then in went the syringe amid muffled howls.

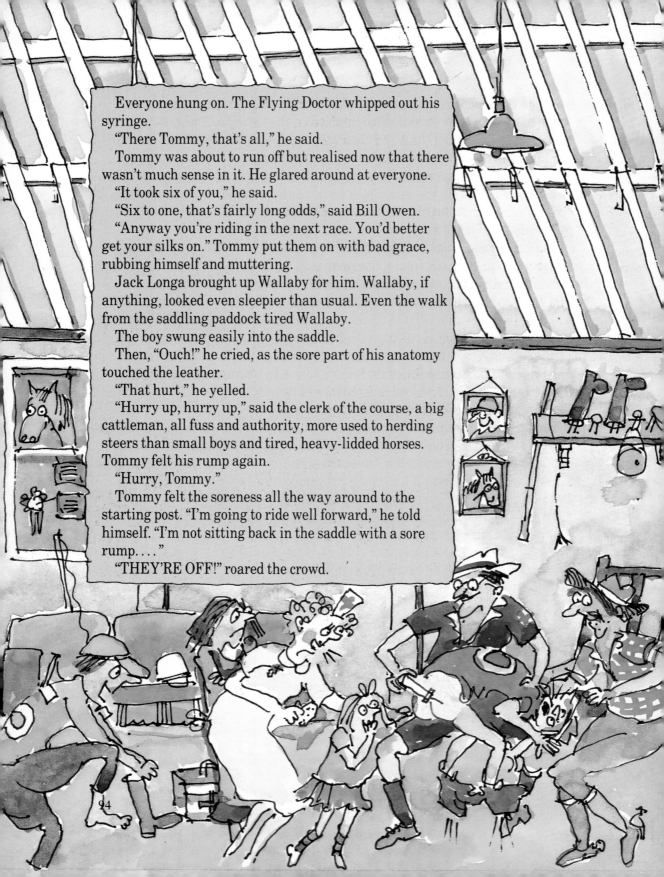

Everyone hung on. The Flying Doctor whipped out his syringe.

"There Tommy, that's all," he said.

Tommy was about to run off but realised now that there wasn't much sense in it. He glared around at everyone.

"It took six of you," he said.

"Six to one, that's fairly long odds," said Bill Owen.

"Anyway you're riding in the next race. You'd better get your silks on." Tommy put them on with bad grace, rubbing himself and muttering.

Jack Longa brought up Wallaby for him. Wallaby, if anything, looked even sleepier than usual. Even the walk from the saddling paddock tired Wallaby.

The boy swung easily into the saddle.

Then, "Ouch!" he cried, as the sore part of his anatomy touched the leather.

"That hurt," he yelled.

"Hurry up, hurry up," said the clerk of the course, a big cattleman, all fuss and authority, more used to herding steers than small boys and tired, heavy-lidded horses. Tommy felt his rump again.

"Hurry, Tommy."

Tommy felt the soreness all the way around to the starting post. "I'm going to ride well forward," he told himself. "I'm not sitting back in the saddle with a sore rump. . . ."

"THEY'RE OFF!" roared the crowd.

Tommy, head down, was last away, the dust of the other horses in his face. He dug his heels in. Nothing happened. Then he sat back in his saddle and something like a knife went through his seat. He gave a scream and then a yell, and the pain launched him forward on to the horse's neck like a bullet.

Old Wallaby liked to take his time. The screams above him and the sudden heavy weight on his neck frightened the few wits he had clean out of his slow old horse's head.

He determined to get away from it and pounded his hooves on the ground, took the bit in his teeth and bolted.

"Go it, Wallaby, look at Wallaby, go it, Wallaby!" screamed the Flying Nurse.

"Go it, Wallaby, go it, boy. Look at 'im!" Jack Longa climbed up on a post.

"Wallaby, Wallaby!" roared the crowd.

Tommy tried to steady Wallaby. He knew the horse would blow himself out. Wallaby was only capable of a short run. He sat back in the saddle again, forgetting . . .

"YEOOOOOOWWWWW," screamed Tommy,
remembering and feeling the pain in his breeches again.
That did it for Wallaby. He flew home, passing horse after
horse, trying to get away from that thing on his neck, his
nostrils wide, foam on his lips, his heels pounding and
dust rising behind him like the tail of a comet.

"Wallaby, Wallaby, Wallaby, Wallaby . . ." roared the
crowd.

They went past the winning post to wild cheers.

Tommy kept going. He was afraid to pull up because
then he'd have to lean back in the saddle again. The clerk
of the course came after him as old Wallaby began to slow
down.

"The race is over lad," he said.

Then Tommy was out of the saddle and walking along, leading Wallaby. "I'm not sitting in that saddle again."

"What happened, boy?" asked the chief steward. "You ran a good race, but you were jerking up and down as if someone had stuck a knife in you."

"Someone did," shouted the boy, pointing at the Flying Doctor. "He did. He gave me an injection."

There was a hushed silence.

The chief steward, who was actually old Bong Booner, the storekeeper, looked serious and stern.

"You mean you were given an injection before the race?"

"Yes, Bong," said the boy. "He did it." The accusing finger again.

"He's been nobbled. The kid's been nobbled," the spectators began shouting. "Disqualify him...."

"Rule Eight says that the hadministering of a drug before a race..." old Bong began pompously.

"Now wait a minute," said the Flying Doctor. "This was an anti-tetanus injection we've been trying to give the boy for days."

"It wasn't one of them henergy drugs to make 'im go faster?" asked Bong, pushing back his big hat and scratching his bald, troubled head.

"It's to safeguard the boy. I've given them to your children, Bong."

The committee went into a huddle. Bong cleared his throat.

"In view of the extenuatin' circumstance, the placings remain."

"Hurray!" cried the crowd. The bar became a roar of noise again. The eagle still wheeled, high and remote.

"Tommy," said the Flying Doctor, "how about a drink on me?"

A moment later they all stood at the soft drink stall. The doctor lifted his drink high and stared around solemnly.

"Well," he said, "I've seen some close finishes in my day, but this is the first time I've seen a race won by a tail!"

Everyone laughed.

And as they drank the toast the Flying Nurse looked mischievous and whispered, "Hey, Tommy, had yer jabs?"

Written by Max Fatchen
Illustrated by Bettina Guthridge

The Valiant Chattee-Maker

Adapted from the Indian folk-tale by **PAT EDWARDS.** Illustrated by **PETER FOST**

> Long, long ago during a violent storm a tiger crept close to the walls of a poor old woman's hut...

*a "chattee-maker" is a potter

But all was far from quiet inside the hut, for the roof was old and leaky.

Drip, drip, drip! Leaks all over the place.

The old woman ran from side to side, dragging first one thing and then another out of the way of the drips. And as she did she grumbled out loud to herself.

Oh dear, oh dear, how frightening this all is. I declare I wouldn't be scared half as much by a tiger as I am by this _perpetual dripping!_

The tiger listened in growing fear.

What can this _perpetual dripping be_, if it frightens an old woman more than I can? It must be something _dreadful!_

99

Inside the old woman fell over her pots and pans that she had set out to catch the drips.

CRASH! BANG! CLATTER!

What a terrible noise! That must be the dreaded *perpetual dripping!*

Just then a chattee-maker who'd been out searching for his runaway donkey came down the road.

Just wait till I catch that good-for-nothing animal.

I'll teach it a lesson!

Now the chattee-maker had been drinking and wasn't quite himself, so when a flash of lightning showed a large animal lying close to the old woman's hut he mistook it for his donkey.

There's my wretched donkey — lying in comfort while I have to hunt through the rain for it!

ext morning the chattee-maker's wife was astounded when she looked out of window. So were the neighbours. And so was the chattee-maker.

> **Amazing!**

> Hey, everyone! Come and see the tiger.

> Husband, come and look at this.

> And to think I thought it was our donkey!

> Would you believe it? A *tiger!*

> The chattee-maker has tied up a tiger outside his house.

> I do hope he won't beat me again!

Gossip being what it is, it wasn't long before the Rajah heard all about the chattee-maker who had caught a tiger and tied it to a post.

> I must meet this man for myself.

The valiant chattee-maker was brought to court and the Rajah heaped honour and wealth upon him

> I admire bravery!

> So, I'm making you a lord in charge of 10 000 horses and you can have some land, three houses and as much money as will fill a well!

> How can I thank you Sire?

> He's getting it the easy way!

> Hush! You'll lose your head!

Much, much later, after the tiger had long gone and the chattee-maker and his wife had got used to being a lord and lady, a neighbouring rajah decided to invade this land. None of the generals wanted to be in charge of defence for fear of losing the battle, knowing it would mean the loss of their heads.

Well come along, which of you is to lead my army into battle?

I'm truly sorry, Sire, but I'll be sick that day.

That was *my* excuse!

I can't do it! My sword is blunt.

I'm losing my voice. *I* can't take command.

I think I'll probably sleep in that day!

I have to go to my grandmother's funeral.

Then someone had a bright idea.

What about the valiant chattee-maker? A man who can tie a tiger to a post would surely make an excellent army commander!

Splendid idea! Send for him at once.

They sent for the chattee-maker and the Rajah appointed him Commander of the Royal Army.

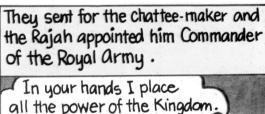

In your hands I place all the power of the Kingdom. You must put our enemies to flight.

The chattee-maker was in despair.

What will I do? What will I **do**?

Oh, stop fussing. Climb up on the horse and I'll tie you on so you won't fall off.

And that's what his wife did.

I don't like this!

Make the knots good and tight.

When the horse felt all the ropes about him, he began rearing and prancing and then set off as fast as he could with the chattee-maker hanging on like grim death.

HELP! HELP!

I must get away!

105

Over hedges, ditches, rivers and plains... away... away... like a flash of lightning, swerving now this way, now that, galloped the horse with the chattee-maker frantically begging it to stop, until *horrors!*..the enemy camp came into sight.

The chattee-maker was desperate, for he knew the enemy would kill him.

I'll grab this tree and maybe the ropes will break, and I can fall off. Better broken bones than an enemy sword!

But the horse was still going at top speed and the soil in which the banyan tree grew was loose, so that when the chattee-maker gave the tree a violent tug it came up by the roots.

The madly frightened horse galloped even faster and the bewildered chattee-maker clung to the tree. All the soldiers in the camp, expecting an army, thought he must be leading a charge against them.

They ran to their Rajah and, gossip being what it is, somehow the story got exaggerated.

107

And so catching is panic, they fled for their lives, pausing only long enough for their Rajah to write a letter calling off the invasion and proposing peace.

Do you spell 'sincerely' with an s or a c?

Put 'Yours truly'. It's shorter!

Be quick, Sire! The ground already shakes from the thundering hooves of the enemy. A huge army is approaching!

They'd barely disappeared when the chattee-maker galloped into the camp.

Heaven help me! I'm a DEAD MAN!

Just at that moment the ropes snapped. The tired horse stopped and the chattee-maker fell to the ground.

Oof!

SNAP.

Puff! Puff!

BOING!

SKIIID!

As soon as he recovered, the chattee-maker looked around the enemy camp and found the letter, so he set off for home — walking this time.

I'll never ride again!

Once home, he told his wife to send the horse back to the Rajah, along with the letter.

Tell them I'll arrive on foot tomorrow.

Excellent idea! Then no one will know you still can't ride.

NEXT MORNING:

See how modest he is. He walks like us instead of riding a horse.

He defeats all our enemies then walks to the palace like a simple man of the people.

THIS WAY TO THE PALACE

Isn't he *wonderful!*

HURRAH FOR THE CHATTEE-MAKER!

And the chattee-maker was rewarded by being made an even greater lord in charge of 20 000 horses, (not one of which he ever rode) and given enough money to fill two wells.

P.S. Are you disappointed the tiger didn't come back into the story? So was I, but alas, this is the way the old tale goes so I didn't like to change it.

109

My Week

MONDAY — wrote novel, two TV plays and a book of light verse. TUESDAY — got up early, had light breakfast (two 50 watt bulbs), swam channel. Back in time to watch Coronation Street. WEDNESDAY — organised and took part in four armed robberies, in Birmingham area. Came home with £250 000. THURSDAY laid low — played with the kids. Wrote second novel. FRIDAY — blackmailed local alderman at lunchtime, went to PTA meeting at night. SATURDAY — sprang two mates from Strangeways. Watched Match of the Day. SUNDAY — two mates came over for dinner. Roast lamb, carrots and turnips, jacket potatoes. Police raid during rice pudding — went quietly.

Roger McGough

Winning Words
Glossary

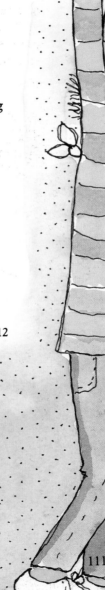

adversary (*p.66*)
opponent

amiability (*p.28*)
friendliness

anatomy (*p.94*)
body

anguish (*p.89*)
mental pain

assuming (*p.63*)
taking for granted

bill-of-fare (*p.47*)
menu

Chancellor (*p.62*)
chief minister

chastened (*p.87*)
behaving themselves
because they had been
punished

conundrum (*p.70*)
a puzzle or riddle

encounter (*p.70*)
face-to-face contest

exhortations (*p.71*)
urgent requests

extenuatin' (*p.97*)
extenuating: excusing

galvanised (*p.93*)
coated with zinc to
prevent it from rusting

humour (*p.32*)
to agree with the
wishes of someone

impartiality (*p.74*)
fairness

in audience (*p.62*)
in a meeting or
interview with
someone

Glossary continues on page 112

Does this mean I can have the rice pudding?

influence (*p.28*)
the power to affect or change things

jollification (*p.75*)
merriment

laconic (*p.89*)
saying a lot in very few words

languid (*p.88*)
limp or slow-moving

lick for leather (*p.88*)
at great speed

lolloped (*p.71*)
ran lazily

nobbled (*p.97*)
drugged

pavilion (*p.64*)
a large and luxurious tent

perpetual (*p.99*)
lasting for ever

rouseabouts (*p.93*)
handymen who work on cattle or sheep stations

scrag (*p.5*)
grab by the throat

spell (*p.90*)
a rest or break

squandered (*p.7*)
wasted

sterling (*p.47*)
excellent

stockwhip (*p.91*)
long leather whip with heavy handle, used for driving the cattle

thermals (*p.93*)
warm air currents

validity (*p.65*)
correctness